*T*EENAGERS often simmer thoughts and feelings without revealing them. Several factors discourage their sharing: they feel misunderstood, our own reactions provoke them to close themselves, they are embarrassed, afraid. Reasons are as numerous as teenagers.

Last winter, Between Us Publishing proposed to thousands of teenagers that they express themselves candidly, reveal themselves to their parents. They were welcome to write with the freedom of anonymity if they chose. Hundreds of teenagers sent us letters; all touched us. We selected as many as we had room for, and are sharing them with you today.

Each of these letters contains a pearl. Sometimes, it shimmers at the beginning, sometimes it waits till the end, when the teenager escapes his or her shell and reveals at last the deep feeling wanting to be shared all along, but which took the writer time to unveil.

I invite you to be open to these teenagers, probably not very different than those you know.

They've already touched more than one reader:

"I was deeply moved. Teenagers, in general, don't like to talk or to be questioned about themselves. They keep many things secret inside. That is why I believe reading letters like these can open parents to the inner life of their children, or at least encourage them to keep trying to establish contact even after many scorned replies and stubborn silences."
        Diane T., mother of a teenage girl and a teenage boy.

"I knew there were teenagers who were going through such emotions, but I didn't think they were so similar to mine. It showed me I wasn't alone!"
        Anna B., teenager

Welcome,

Sonia Bahl
Publisher

Between Us Publishing inc.

United States:
90 Patterson Road
Worthington, MA, 01098

Canada:
2145 Alfred Street   **Phone: (514) 526-3283**
Brossard (Quebec)   **Fax: (514) 879-8335**
J4Z 1G4   **Internet / E-mail: bahl@cam.org**

Revisions: **David R. Southwick**
Graphic concept: EKHO DESIGNS ENR.
Illustrations: Rene Bourassa, Chantal Decelles, Elaine Despins,
          Marilou Giroux, Nicolas L'Heureux, Patrick Laviolette,
          Shadi Mallak, Isabelle Philip, Mariette Tome , Debra Yee.

ISBN 1-896650-00-7

Library of Congress Catalog Card Number: 95-83089

Legal Deposit — Bibliothèque nationale du Québec, 1996
          National Library of Canada, 1996

Canadian Cataloguing in Publication Data
Main entry under title:

Dear parents

(Series Letters)
Issued also in French under title: Chers parents.
Letters of teenagers to parents.

ISBN 1-896650-00-7

1. Parent and teenager. 2. Teenagers . 3. Teenagers'writings.
I. Series.

HQ799.15.C4413   1996   306.874   C95-941587-4

DISTRIBUTED BY I.P.G., Chicago, Illinois
To order: Phone: (800) 888-4741
                    (312) 337-0747
          Fax: (312) 337-5985
          E-mail: ipgbook@mcs.com

Printed in Canada

Dear **parents**

Between Us Publishing inc.

Dear parents,

I am writing you this letter to share my despair. Ever since I was very young, you have taught me to respect others, to tell the truth and to share, yet these days, you do exactly the opposite of what you taught me. I am very disappointed in you. Your fights wear me down. You have no respect for each other. You are only interested in finding a crutch, a life-saver. Blaming each other won't bring your daughter back. She's dead. Often you seem to forget that she was my sister. I also felt like I'd killed her, but she simply wanted to stop suffering. She was hurting inside, she was choking. The only person she confided in was me, and I didn't see her pain. How do you think I feel? For a long time, I blamed myself. I was filled with remorse, and I thought about closing my eyes permanently, too. But instead, I went looking for people who helped me to see that it wasn't my fault, or anyone else's. I'm asking you once again, GET HELP. Feeling sorry for yourselves won't pull you out of this.

Mom, you don't sleep, you don't eat, and you don't even have the heart to go on your daily walk. You spend your days crying in Audrey's room, smelling her clothes and looking at pictures of her.

And you Dad, you get up to go to work, yet your eyes are empty of life. When you come home, you sit in front of the TV until sleep surprises you.

But me, I am still alive and I need you. PLEASE GET HELP! Do it for me, your son, who can't stand watching you sink into darkness any further. I love you from the bottom of my heart.

Your son,

Phil

Hello you two,

Listen carefully, because I'm finally going to talk about it. I don't know how to say it, but I know how to write it: I LOVE YOU! These three words are very easy to think, but are really hard to say. Yet I know you understand me... eh, Dad? I never say it to you, but you don't tell me that you love me either. An unconscious feeling joins us together and we both know that we love each other. With you Mom, it's jokingly that you say it: "Oh, I DO love you sometimes." It's the "sometimes" I like.

I must point out that it's true that I'm not always lovable. But, anyway, I wonder why those words so easily spoken in other families are so hard to say in ours?

It's not that I don't try, on the contrary. I try in every way possible, in every way imaginable. I say "Mom, would you come to my room and talk to me, while I'm picking up and putting stuff away?" This really means: "Mom, I need to be with you, to have your attention." Dad, when I ask you how to check the oil in the car, or how to change a flat tire, it's not to bug you, but to get your attention too. It's also a roundabout way of being with you, so you can teach me things. I don't know why, but I need you to teach me things.

Now let's talk about overprotection. Yes, for some teens, overprotection is something that drives them crazy, but for me it's proof of your love. By the way, Mom, you always make me laugh when you come outside to tell me: "Have a good night. Be careful. Take care of yourself, and don't forget, be careful!" And I answer you coldly "Yeah, yeah, Mom... don't worry!" Even if it doesn't look like it, I feel that's proof of your love.

In fact, I'm writing this letter to express a feeling that's been hiding inside me for a long time, and that boils down to: I LOVE YOU! Why not say it openly anyway? Let's forget about being embarrassed, and speak our feelings, once and for all!

Your turtledove,

Ellen

Dear parents,

It's difficult for me tonight to sit down and write to you. How could I tell you in a single letter all the things I usually am unable to say to you. Everything I have in my heart could suddenly be released and explode like a time bomb, because of too many emotions being held back for so long. But if you knew... if you could but guess at all the emotions and contradictory feelings that attack me... all these fears, apprehensions, hopes and doubts, that too often I cover up. If you only knew how confused I am sometimes and how I have trouble finding myself, how afraid I am so often of not meeting your standards! Understand, I really want you to always be proud of me. But then, I know what you think. You believe adolescence is the wild age, that we teenagers don't know what we want, that we're careless. But it's not true! It's just that we're kind of victims of our drive to out-do ourselves and keep living new experiences. We're also at an age where our ideas, our values and our goals in life are frequently questioned. Maybe now you see the reasons for my changes in attitude. I also think about the life that awaits me. It's so full of

mystery, it makes my head spin. So many hopes, aspirations, plans, and ideas keep coming to me. I want to do everything, but my means are limited. I would not forgive myself if I forget about all the traps that life sets in front of me; that's why I need you, to help me find my way and support me during difficult moments, because my lack of experience could easily lead to defeat or failure. I also need you to help me reach for my full potential each day.

Even though it often seems bitter, we love life and want to make the most of it. Let's just hope that one day we will successfully build this ideal world we all want, even though so many have already given up. In conclusion, I want to say thank you... thank you for this life that you are giving me.

Keith

Dear parents,

Stop for thirty seconds and listen to me. When I come home from school, I'm alone. When I want to share my joys, I'm alone. When I need to be comforted, I'm alone. You're always out. You've either gone to work or are out having a good time. What about me in all this? You've never thought about me! I escape to friends' homes where shouts, discussions and laughter fill the house. But when I go home, the emptiness is even greater. It can be so pervasive. If only you knew how lonely I feel. I can't stand it anymore, I need you to be here.

Clark

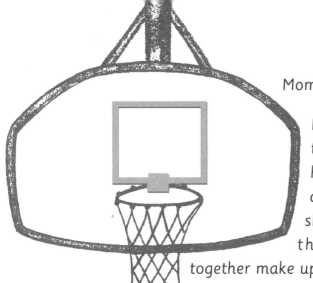

Mom, Dad,

In my heart for a long time, I have felt anger, hatred and sadness, alternating like sunshine and rain. These three emotions put together make up another one: despair. Despair at never being loved as much as I would like, hopelessness at always being rejected and never being understood.

In the middle of all that, secretly, I'm sending you a distress signal that you don't seem to hear, despite my efforts.

I scream out in the night, a scream that breaks open my heart and releases the anger, hate and sadness that make up my despair.

Chris

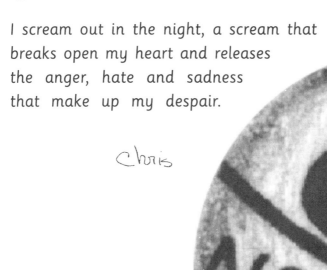

Dear Dad,

I'm writing to you because it seems like we never have time to talk. I also think it's not always easy for you and me to talk. I don't know where to start. I love you more than anyone in the world, but I have trouble showing you.

I feel like you want me to be perfect... You want me to like what you like, and do what you do. I don't like sports. I must have gotten that from Mom. I can't be a really good student and be really well-behaved at school. It's not easy to go to a private school.

Patrick, why claim Patrick is my brother when I don't even know him? You never talk to me about him. I think you and my half-brother are great buddies. Why can't you be the same with me? I know I'm younger than he is and I'm a girl, and when he was my age, you didn't see him. I can't wait to see what you'll be like with me when I'm his age. I wonder what you'd say if you knew I was doing drugs. I wonder too what you'd do if I brought you home another grandson when I was only 17, like your DARLING SON did. Mom doesn't have to accept the child you had with another woman, twenty years ago. It's hard for her too. Do you talk to her any more than you talk to me?

It might not be obvious but I'm not that stupid. Just because I'm young doesn't mean I don't have any feelings.

There's another thing I can't forgive you for: why did you separate me from my best friend when we were little? She and I, we were like sisters, and then suddenly we couldn't speak to each other anymore. Why?

I wrote to your sister because, like me, she had a silent father. I didn't know Gramps, but to hear others talk, you are just like him: serious, hard-working, peaceful, and you never let your feelings show. It makes me mad because I never know if you're happy, sad or angry. Consequently, I never know how to talk to you.

I love you Dad! Mom gives me affection, but I need some from you too. When I needed to be taught new things, you were never there, you never had time.

I end this letter by saying I love you sincerely. I'd like us to talk. Have we ever talked about anything other than school or your work? Could we talk about our feelings? I need you as much as I need Mom. You can never make up for the times you weren't with Patrick. You often buy me lots of things, but material things don't replace the love of a father.

I love you! If, like me, you can't voice your feelings, write to me. Please communicate. All I want is to really know you.

Your loving daughter,

Nancy

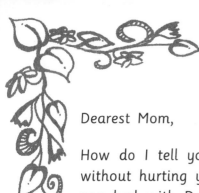

Dearest Mom,

How do I tell you what's been going on in my head, without hurting you or losing you? Ever since the fight you had with Dad, when you told him you wanted to kill yourself, I'm scared. I'm scared because I know very well that you could do it. You've lived through so much pain and sadness that I understand your reaction. But, see, I'm still the little girl who needs her mom. Remember all the magical moments we've spent together, all the tears we've shed together, all the secrets we've whispered in each other's ears? It makes me happy to recall all the precious memories you are part of.

What I'm trying to make you understand is that you are important to me and I love you from the bottom of my heart. I will always be there for you, even in the hardest times. When you love someone, you stay with that person and support her emotionally in happy times and in hard times, right? All I'm asking is for you to believe me when I say things will work out eventually. And please don't kill yourself (if you can't stay alive for yourself, do it for your two sons and me). Suicide is not a good way to escape, even though you may believe it is at the moment. If only you knew how much life is worth living!

I hope these few words will make you think, and that you will make the right decision. No matter what happens, don't ever forget that I love you.

Your little girl, who doesn't want to lose you,

Goldie

Dear Mom and Dad,

This is the hardest thing I've ever had to tell someone. It's hard to tell you because, I don't know how you'll react, and I don't know if you'll still love me after I tell you. The thing I need to tell you is that I'm gay. It's just that I had to tell you, it was tearing me apart. It's one of those things I just can't explain how I feel on the inside. I kind of know how you feel, it's kind of like when you're a little kid and you hear that there's no such thing as Santa Clause, you feel disappointment, and your expectations die, but you get over it. I hope you do the same for me and get over it. Every night that I couldn't tell you was a living hell, I would lie awake at night and wonder if you would still love me after I tell you.

Your loving son,

Robert

Dear parents,

I can't stop myself from reliving the day that I first met him. He was 60 and I was only 14. He seemed to be nice and friendly. He ran a busy corner store. At the time, I was just a customer. I soon realized this man was trying to get closer to me as best he could. I'll call him Leon. I can't help thinking about everything that happened before I realized this man wanted more than my friendship. Let me explain.

Everything started one night when he wanted to talk. Calmly, I told him not to get worked up and not to be shy, he could tell me everything. Little did I know that he wanted to betray the friendship we had started. I didn't know he was capable of taking from me everything I had. After this discussion, where he wasn't being honest, I tried to avoid him. Several weeks later, he told me he needed someone to help him wash his coolers. I will never forget the moment when he quietly approached me and patted my butt a couple of times.

At once, I was appalled but, in spite of that, I took it all. Suddenly, I felt as if life had let me down. I couldn't stop thinking of what this man had taken from me. He took away the pleasure of feeling loved. For a while, I thought life had nothing more to offer me, so I let myself consider certain alternatives. Then I started to avoid him again. But he seemed to change. So I decided to act as if nothing had happened. Don't forget that he was my best friend's grandfather. Time passed, and soon it was time for me to leave. I then realized he would have liked to keep me with him.

When I came back for summer courses, I couldn't help but see him again. I thought and thought about everything he had put me through. At the end of my summer courses, it was time for me to leave again. My friend was working at the corner store, so before leaving, I decided to go see her to chat. Suddenly, I realized I'd accidentally forgotten something useful for traveling in the office where Leon was napping. I summoned up all my courage and, very quietly, walked into his office, making as little noise as possible so as not to wake him. In spite of my efforts, he woke up anyway. I tried to get away from him, but he took me in his arms, telling me I was his "baby" and his love, and that he would miss me. At that moment, I knew I should escape, but I was paralyzed. No part of my body seemed to want to move. I was appalled when he kissed me, but again I took it all.

Afterwards, I left, still shaking, without even saying a word to my friend. Two days later, I had no time at all to think of him because I had so many things to do. Still, I couldn't help thinking that I'd soon have to go back.

Work went well. Three weeks later, I was already packing up to go back to this merciless man. I can't forget the day of my arrival. I thought he had changed. And yet, he was looking at me, and talking to me in the same way he had before, as if nothing had happened in his office before I had left. I continued to act normally until the day of my birthday. He decided to give me a present. To me, the gift made me think he now had absolute power over me. His gift was a hundred dollar bill. I immediately thought he was trying to buy me. With this gift, he also gave me a card, where he explained how much he loved me.

I barely stopped myself from crying. I ran home to scream and cry quietly in my own world. A week later, I was unable to keep this secret anymore, it was too heavy for me. I decided to talk to my brother about it. I knew he was the only one at home who could help me. I wasn't wrong. He let me cry and talk, and then he gave me advice. He said I should give the money back and tell Leon that I couldn't accept it. When I told my brother I didn't want to go alone, he said he would come with me. Armed with my courage, I went to return the money that I couldn't take. My brother waited for me outside.

I went into the corner store, gave him back his money, saying that I couldn't take it. He asked me then to explain further but I said nothing. As I was leaving, he said that one of these days we would have to talk.

I left the store and went to find my brother, who was hiding in the yard. We returned home and I tried to forget Leon. Usually, after school was the time I would stop at his store. But he soon figured out I was trying to avoid him. It was two months before I started going back. And then only with my friend. Since then, I go there only for emergencies or when I'm with my friend.

Now I'm 16, nearly 17. It's been almost three years that I've put up with him. Now he doesn't come too close to me, and he leaves me alone. I want to end this letter by thanking you for listening to me. Don't worry, I'm safe now. I would just like you to stop thinking that your daughter has no problems. On the contrary, I have as many as you do. Only, I try to hide them.

Jade

Dear parents,

What can I say to you? I can only thank you for everything you've done for me. For nearly fifteen years, you've fed and sheltered me in your house, and no doubt you will continue to do so for a few more years. I am very grateful. I know I can never repay you.

I feel so ungrateful: I don't deserve the happiness you offer me. You've worked hard, and have guided me, so I could have a better life than you did. But all this is in vain, because I'm a worthless idiot. Why, why can't I study like others do and succeed as they do?

When I get my tests back in school, I can only remain speechless with envy and shame, while others brag about their marks. What do they have that I don't? I'm always asking myself this same question. What can I tell you? What excuses do I have to justify my marks?

Maybe you weren't hard enough on me? Maybe you are too demanding? Or am I the problem? What can I do to help myself and to please you? All these questions have lingered in my heart for a long time and torment me. I shudder every time I ponder on one of those questions. I'm scared, scared of what could happen to me in the future. All the possibilities frighten me. When I look towards the future, based on what I've accomplished so far, I see only a hole, a deep black hole, so dark I can barely see myself.

I'm desperate... I don't think I'll ever succeed, because I don't have what it takes. There's always a solution to every problem. If I don't find one soon, maybe I'll have to consider drugs or suicide...

Your son,

Paul

My dear mother,

So many years have come and gone since the stormy night when you packed your bags. I can still picture that night; I stood by the door, watching you leave with that tall man, keeping myself from holding on to you. You left without thinking about us. Don't you love us? Our love wasn't strong enough to hold you.

It must be fifteen years since you left, you didn't see me grow up. Dad... has aged a great deal. Every year, April 24, I see him in his best suit, sitting at the table where he has lit candles and poured two glasses of wine, waiting for you... but every year, I see him in despair. The holidays, when everyone celebrates with their families, are the saddest days for us, because we have memories of the happy days with you. You spoiled us with your surprises and your gentle caresses. But where did my beloved mother, who used to tell me that she loved me more than anything in the world, go?

I will be eighteen soon and I still don't understand why you left two people you loved so, for someone who you barely knew. You always told me not to talk to strangers because they might be big bad wolves, so why did you follow a big bad wolf who stole you away from us? Does he mean more to you than your own flesh and blood? Not too long ago I saw you at a mall, but I did not dare call to you because I was afraid you wouldn't recognize me. I followed you while you did your shopping. How you have aged! Your hands are no longer smooth as they were when you caressed my fore-head, and you have lost so much weight. Does he treat you well? If not, would you come back to us like before? We are all impatiently waiting for you! We love you mom!

Your daughter who loves you and misses you,

Vanessa

Dear parents,

Today I hope with all my heart that you can understand everything there is in my thoughts and in my heart. I would like to have the comfort of your words and your hugs. I feel cut off, misunderstood, and questions keep dancing in my head.

I want to ask dad first: Why do you react so negatively when I state my opinions, my dreams, and my ideas? Why don't you listen to me when I say that something's wrong?! And tell me, why ignore me when all I want is a little comfort, and to be listened to and understood? Speak to me, speak to me! Why does it seem so easy for others?! I have lots of love to give, but I need some for myself too. Why don't we talk, and get to know each other better? The treats and all the stuff you can give me, I don't want it. I want you to hug me and talk to me; tell me about your day, your fears, your sadness, your dreams, and the hopes you keep inside. Right now I am trying to get to you, but one day it will be you who needs me. I am not ten years old anymore and pretty soon I will be an adult. I will leave home and you will never have the chance to know me. I love you and I know that you love me too, but I beg you

to think about what I am saying. As for me, I am ready to do anything to bring us together, because you are precious to me.

And you mom, so understanding, so gentle, so nice, how do you manage to love us, talk to us, and be so in touch with us? I would like to do special things with you, and get to know you other than as a mother. Other kids want to travel, go out into the world and do all kinds of things. But I have traveled with my mother: I've closed my eyes and let the warmth of the hollow of her heart cradle me as if I were floating on a cloud. Thank you for all the little lessons of life you shared with me.

To get back to what I am asking of you, I really only want understanding, respect and your trust. I hope you will understand, or else these thoughts will go unheard in your heart.

Sincerely, your child who just wants to say "I love you."

John

Dear Dad,

You've probably noticed that I haven't been quite the same in a while. I cry a lot and I hardly talk to you anymore. Some days, I don't feel like doing anything, I feel like letting myself die. I'm writing to you because I have a huge problem and I need you to help me figure out what to do. I know that when you'll hear what it is, you'll probably be mad at me for a long time. Maybe I deserve it – I don't know. What I do know is that I really need you. You've often told me not to tell you if this ever happened, because I'd regret it. But you see, I can't keep this to myself any longer. It's killing me, it hurts so much. I'm scared of what you'll think of me, the daughter you've always trusted, but if you believe in me, you'll understand. I don't want you to react right away. Please take the time to think. I certainly don't want you to worry to death about me. I will be responsible. I'm old enough to do that. You're the person I trust the most because I love you so much. That's why I've decided to tell you in spite of what you've said to me. You know, if I didn't tell you, I would feel as though I was deceiving you. I'm tired of keeping this to myself. It's a heavy secret, too heavy to carry alone.

Dad, I'm pregnant. I hope that when you read this, you won't get too mad at me. I know it's hard, but you must help me get through this. You must understand that this is just as hard for me as it is for you. Your support is vital to me. Remember when I was a little girl, you were always there for me. Whether I was having problems with school or with my friends, you always helped me get through them. When I found myself without friends, you did everything you could to make me feel better. Remember that you told me you'd be there for me. If you let me down, I think I'll die. I've known for two months. The father doesn't know yet, and I don't think I'll have the guts to tell him. Actually, I really don't want him to know. I don't want this baby. I won't be able to look after it, to bring it up or even love it and, worst of all, I don't love the father anymore.

You'll think I'm irresponsible, that I'm acting like a child, and you're right: I still am a little girl, and I'm not ready for this kind of responsibility. The baby would be miserable with me. I just want you to understand that I really need you because when I'm with you, I feel good. I've never felt this bad in my entire life. I think this is the worst thing that could happen to a girl my age. It's the life of a human being that we have inside, and its life depends on our decision. If you think I'm making the right decision, then you understand me, because life is something very precious and very fragile. Its life rests in my hands. I know what you must be feeling at this moment, and what I hope for most in the world is that you're not thinking about what you've already told me. I know this letter goes on forever, but I have so many feelings I want to share with you. I'd like to be a little girl again like when you used to hold me in your arms and hug me when I was sad.

I wonder why parents change so much. You're less understanding. You're around when we have little problems, but when they get serious, you hide as if to protect yourselves. I don't understand that at all. This is not a reproach, just a question. Mom wouldn't understand this, so that's why I'm telling you. I could have had an abortion, and pretended nothing had ever happened, but I think it's wrong to do that. What I hope for the most in the world is that you will be there tonight, and that when I get home you will hug me tight. I'm scared. I'm really scared. I feel powerless, and I'll say this again and again: without you, I'm nothing. The life of this child rests in my hands like my life rests in yours. So I'm asking you only one thing: help me, because I really need you. We'll be two to face this anguish. It will be shared and it will be a bond between us forever. I think it would be the greatest proof of love you could ever give me.

I'm saying good-bye, hoping you will understand.

I love you, Dad, from your daughter,

Sallie

Dad,

Should I call you dad, or use your first name? This is a confusing dilemma. You are both my biological creator and a deceitful stranger. You gave me life, and then, when I was four years old, you took it away from me. Since then I have never seen you again. I now have a chance to tell you what

I feel. When you went away it left me bruised. Maybe I was too young to understand what you were doing to mom, but I was old enough to be imprinted by your hateful, demented acts. Instead of being full of admiration and love, I have an immeasurable rage burning in my heart, and it will last till I die. Even if your jealousy and violence were due to your so-called alcoholism, you never laid a hand on me, violent or affectionate. Yet the pain you inflicted on mom left a deep impression on me. For that, I will hate you forever.

When mom read me fairy tales, I compared the princess to mom and the horrible monster to you. Isn't it ironic of me to compare a monster to a monster?

You had quite an impact, father. Your departure was not without its consequences. I have suffered them: nocturnal hallucinations, confusion, androphobia, nightmares, insecurities. And one incurable fear: I was afraid of you. Is it normal to be afraid of your own father? The mention of your name scared me. You disgusted me. For a long time, I was consumed with help-lessness. Today my fear has evapo-rated and has been replaced by revulsion. Consider yourself lucky that mom has recovered from her long, painful suffering. Consider yourself lucky that she isn't a bitter, vengeful

Nemesis. She forgives you. I don't. But like me, she will never forget. Despite my hatred, we are bound by blood, father. In the past, you had the chance to love and be loved instead of beating and dominating. I would have given you that chance, the chance to start over. Alas! You decided to flee in secret, like a cowardly little animal. I am convinced that it was for the best. From now on, you will never be anything but a distasteful memory: the memory of a hostile, selfish, loathsome man.

Thank you, dad. Thanks for everything. May God forgive you for your many sins, because I will never be able to.

Your son,

Dear parents,

I imagine the word "dear" appearing at the beginning of this letter, has gotten your attention and your reeling minds are now deeply perplexed. You are vacillating between a state of shock and coma? Great! I guess I've gotten your attention. Would it be too much to ask, for once, for you to notice something other than your own navels and listen to what YOUR DAUGHTER has to say? I've had it up to here with your never-ending sermons about my blue hair. I'm tired of your flow of anger that runs adrift on my confusion. Stop curbing my freedom. Stop criticizing me all the time. Stop yelling at me for stupid reasons! Can't you see you're hurting me? The thought that I could be hurting, too, has obviously never crossed your mind!

I don't even dare imagine what you think of me. Let me tell you: your "good-for-nothing" daughter, as you so nicely call me, is fighting tooth and nail to carve out her own place in this crappy society. My whole damn life I've struggled to make sense of my existence, to believe in something; in short, to be worth more than the idiot I dare to be. My below-zero self-esteem is the fruit of your indifference and your insults. You unjustly accuse me of never doing anything around the house: why don't you start by being there before you bombard me with accusations?! Stop wondering what you've done to the Good Lord (who is he anyway?) to deserve such a druggie as your only daughter, and start wondering instead what led me to do this in the first place.

My soul aches, my heart aches, I ache from hating. I'm searching for myself but I am lost. I want to find self-respect, but I can't. I want to love passionately, but no one has ever shown me how! Forgive me for my ignorance, but that pathetic feeling we have the nerve to call love, does it still exist? Has it ever existed? I doubt it when I look at this dead planet, this sick society. I can't continue my search, dear parents, my suffering has deadened my mind. Allow me before leaving to shed a few tears in memory of your scorn, and please don't hold this against me. Anyway it's too late, I already feel my life slipping away. Good-bye.

Jessica

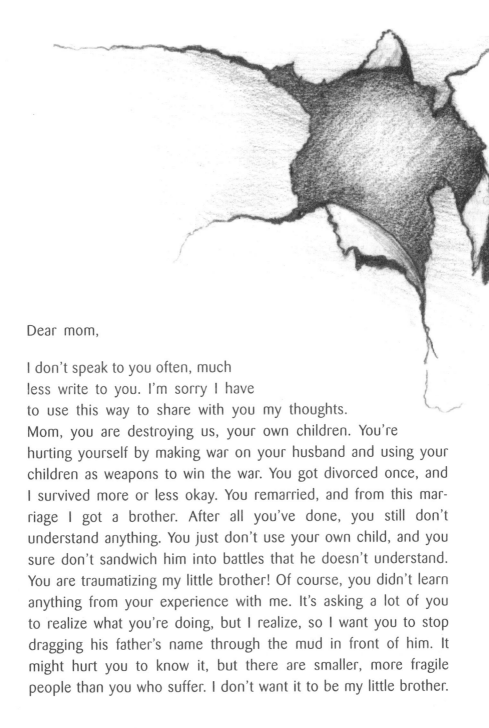

Dear mom,

I don't speak to you often, much
less write to you. I'm sorry I have
to use this way to share with you my thoughts.
Mom, you are destroying us, your own children. You're
hurting yourself by making war on your husband and using your
children as weapons to win the war. You got divorced once, and
I survived more or less okay. You remarried, and from this marriage I got a brother. After all you've done, you still don't
understand anything. You just don't use your own child, and you
sure don't sandwich him into battles that he doesn't understand.
You are traumatizing my little brother! Of course, you didn't learn
anything from your experience with me. It's asking a lot of you
to realize what you're doing, but I realize, so I want you to stop
dragging his father's name through the mud in front of him. It
might hurt you to know it, but there are smaller, more fragile
people than you who suffer. I don't want it to be my little brother.

Maxwell

Dear Parents,

One day, you said to me: "When you are older, you'll understand what we mean..." Well, I'm older now! But I'm not sure I understand life and its innuendoes, fear... Or maybe it's just that I don't want to understand. The future is uncertain, and I feel lost, as if I were all alone in the middle of a field of wheat and the only color I can see all around me is gold... Except that it's a black cloud that haunts my mind: dark fears, dark confusions, dark uncertainties...

I would have liked to stay a child. When I was little, I lived for the day I would become an adult. I always ran faster than time. Even though I'm now out of breath, time won't stop. It won't let me catch up with it. Time has even succeeded in getting ahead of me... Just like my life. Sometimes, it gets beyond me too. I don't know anymore which path to take. I'm 17 and at a crossroads, the most important intersection I'll ever have to cross. And here I am, young and carefree, moving naively forward on this road paved by indifference, individualism, and materialism.

Sometimes, I'm also proud. Proud simply of being who I am, even though I haven't always felt this way, but also proud of my origins. Those who fought for our people, our liberty, and our way of life fill me with pride. They are the ones who give me the will to go forward, to ever surpass myself and to never give in to discouragement.

It is said that the ghosts of childhood follow us for our whole lives, unless of course we exorcise them. I don't think I've exorcised mine yet. Feelings of shame and inferiority still live in my heart. It's hard to talk about them, you feel even more vulnerable when you do. Pain is nevertheless healed by suffering! Maybe I've had enough of suffering, maybe I just want to forget. But one doesn't forget simply because one wishes to.

> *The bitter laugh of rage is now good form*
> *And I, a poet, must eat scorn for food.*
> *I have a heart but am not understood,*
> *Except in moonlight and in great nights of storm.*

So wrote Nelligan. One day I recopied those lines into my journal because they had touched my soul deeply. I understood so well what he was going through! I felt exactly the way he did. Alone, isolated in an indifferent and scornful world.

But unlike Nelligan, a poet I revere, I sincerely believe life is beautiful and that snow eventually melts. All you need is to be really determined, to hang on fervently. Then one day, you realize everything has changed, that you have changed and, yes, that you are happy!

I think it's important to have goals in life, to be dizzy with projects. You must dream, and never stop wanting, because this unbearable ambition pushes you to give the best of yourself, to make the most of your best and richest qualities. You know, I have tons of ambition. It's strange, since there are lots of things in life that make me feel insecure. But when it concerns my future, I have no doubts. I know I will succeed in spite of all the obstacles that may get in my way. Maybe it's only an old dream that I've begun to believe in and that has become, with time, a potential reality. One thing is sure: I'm confident in my future!

More than thirty years separate me from you. Sometimes I have trouble believing that you were once young and sensitive; that your forehead, now furrowed by wrinkles of worry, was once smooth like the water of a lake at dusk. But the older I get, and the more I glimpse fragments of your past, the more I feel close to you. And then I wonder if, by the irony of fate, I won't make the same mistakes you did. I don't want to tie myself down at twenty-five to the security of a stable job. But I don't want to wander like a gypsy until divine Providence chooses my destiny either.

In fact, I don't know what I want! Maybe I do want to be tied down… while holding the key to my freedom?

One day, you're happy. The next, you're sad. This is a bit what I've wanted you to feel throughout my letter. I'd like to be able to find a nice, poetic sentence to express my affection for you. But there's no shower of stars in my mind, nor crackling fire. There are ashes, instead, today. An extinguished fire. But each of these ashes of life blows an "I love you." to those who, having once loved, gave life to them.

Dear parents,

Sometimes, you'd like to help me and know what torments my soul. But you can barely get a word out of me, though I could spend hours telling you my joys, my sorrows, my ambitions. All the things I'd like to express that are proof of my affection, my admiration and my tenderness - the things that stay stuck in my throat - these are the things I'll write down in this letter. Then I will roll it up, put it in a bottle and toss it in the sea!

Four years ago, I was thirteen. According to you, I'd always worked hard in school. I had been in grade eight for three months, and I was losing my grip. Before, you used to say I was generally an easygoing child, happy, sociable, accommodating and athletic. But none of that counted anymore: "That boy's gotten lazy. If he keeps this up, he'll never amount to anything..." "Anxious? Oh no, of course not, no worries, he tells us everything."

"BULLSHIT!" I'd say.

Actually, I was kind of shy, I slept badly, and I still hadn't acquired the "method." I was scared to talk about important things, and you knew that very well. That year, I let my classmates beat me up and never complained. When I fought back, I wasn't as clever as they were. I was always the one getting in trouble, even though they had started it. So in grade eight, I acquired the reputation and the title of trouble-maker, though I was the one being beaten up.

You tried your best to help me, but you didn't really know what to do. Now when I think back, it seems funny. Mom, I have a clear picture in my mind of you reading psychology books to find the solution to my problems. This vision blurs into clouds of words, ideas, fragments of sentences, feelings: anger, misunderstanding, Freud, child psychoanalysis from 5 to 15 years, maturing, development, etc.

Whenever I got my report card, you gave me the same lecture, with the same reproaches: "You don't work hard enough, you're irresponsible and careless, you don't pay enough attention, you make a lot of mistakes." As you already know, the report card always came with teachers' comments: "A little too young. Has good potential, but doesn't know how to use it. Does not work hard enough, etc." I've always thought those comments had a double meaning. What do they mean when they say "A little too young"? How could you be taken in by those comments and criticisms?

You were so sure I was the kind of kid who was contrary and passive, that I had a classic case of laziness, that I just didn't want to work. Many just assumed it was a character deficiency, easily corrected with SMACKS AND PUNISHMENT. What a generalization!

What a stereotype! What a load of CRAP! I had stored up so much anger without ever letting it show. I was so wound up, so tense, that I'd taken to chewing my nails until they bled, and cracking my knuckles, so I wouldn't explode. You used to say to me "Stop eating your nails!" I wanted so much to say something, to yell at you "Go to hell! Get lost! You! School! The whole planet!" But I held back, instead staring you down with hate. My eyes said a lot...

After all I've said and am about to say, you may think I'm ungrateful, that I'm throwing a temper tantrum, boiling over, griping, kicking up a fuss for nothing. But it's all true. I was screaming and screaming my pain, but nobody heard me, no one answered! Except for Grandma, among all the people who gave me advice and scoldings. She was a wonderful woman, the only one to offer me a hand to pull me out of the shadows. Before she passed away, she whispered in my ear: "Let time take care of this. You'll see, everything will work out."

Now, things have changed, and Grandma was right. In spite of everything I may have said and thought, I thank you both, Mom and Dad. I ask for your forgiveness, because even during the hardest times, you never abandoned me. I realize how much I owe you and will always owe you, because you love me and I love you too.

Your son,

Alex

Dear Mom and Dad,

Thanks to this letter, I will finally be able to tell you what I really think, without inter- ruptions and without having to get you together. I want to talk to you about something that happened twelve years ago and that concerns you both.

A long time ago, a four-year-old girl watched two adults, her parents, argue. A few months later, after many such fights, unable to stand it any longer, they mutually decide to break the link that had kept them together for three years. Without any real understanding of the situation, that little girl will have to stay alone with one parent. It will be her mother. That child, dear parents, is Me, your daughter, who learned the word "divorce" before even knowing what "loving" meant. I'm not trying in any way to make you feel guilty for that decision. I now think it was for the best. Growing up, I came to understand and get used to this lifestyle.

Before I understood the reasons for your divorce, I despera- tely wanted to blame someone, and I chose the person I didn't have the opportunity to get to know or understand: my father. I hated him, disowned him, accused him... I didn't want to see him anymore, because, to my way of thinking, I no longer had a father! To survive this void, which I refused to acknowledge, I tried as hard as I could to get other people to love me. So, in an artificial way, I lived happily without my father. The hardest part was that each time I had to leave those other people. So I became more and more emo- tionally fragile. Plus, I had to live with your tears, your complaints and your fits of anger, Mom! I couldn't stand hearing you talk about him, because for me, he was dead. His name was always coming out of your mouth, and it made me sick. The more you talked, the more you made me hate him. From then on, I hated him not because of the divorce, but because of the way he had taken over your mind. Later, I finally recognized that you would never forget him. That was hard for me! You, Dad, were much too absent. Sometimes, I felt you had forgotten me. Even though I didn't want to see you, I still wanted to feel loved. I don't resent you, after all, despite everything.

Now sixteen years old, that little girl from the past has a bit more experience and understands things that were beyond her then. Mom, I accept the fact that you think of him, but I want you to know that you are the one who loved him, not me. I love him instinctively, as a daughter loves her father... nothing more! Dad, I accept as well that you're starting to want to see me and get to know me. But it's hard because you scare me a little. I consider you a stranger. I even have trouble calling you "Dad." It's because I've only seen you about ten times in twelve years.

If I could start over and get you back together, I don't think I would do it because I'm happy with this life even though some moments are harder than others. I've gotten used to my life in a single-parent family. I'm happy with you, Mom. There are advantages to this way of life: I don't need to get the consent of two parents! It can be a good life! I wouldn't want my situation to change for anything in the world, because I've been living like this since I was very young. Many of the best and most important moments in my life happened after your divorce...

Valerie

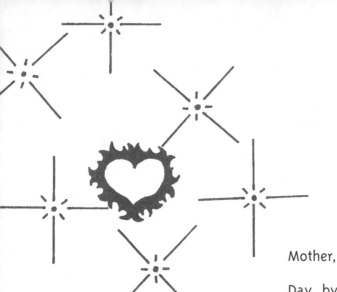

Mother,

Day by day, hour by hour, minute by minute, you're always there for me. Every day that passes you teach me the way to go. You never stop helping me. Even though you sometimes don't understand me (my feelings), you still try your best. I know that every time you guide and help me I forget to say thank you. I never say "I love you." either. It's just that when you love a person as much as I love you, you automatically assume that the loved one knows how you feel. I now know that's not the case. People need to hear it to believe it. Well... I am saying "I love you." and "Thank you." now for everything you have done for me and for everything you will do for me in the future (just in case, I forget to say it at that point!). I just thought I'd tell you how much I appreciate you.

Love always,

Steliana

Dear Parents,

Sometimes you don't understand me. What I wear, how I talk, and the things I worry about may perplex you.

I have to admit, I don't completely understand myself either, much less you.

Life is a lot of give and take, so I need you to make allowances every now and then. But I need boundaries, too, so that I don't abuse my freedom.

Let me talk on the phone for an hour once in a while. Forbid me to drink. Allow me to choose my own wardrobe. Prohibit the use of cigarettes. Permit me to go on a "hot date" Saturday night. Encourage me to abstain from sex. And please, dear mom and dad, make sure you warn me about the fine line between right and wrong. Help me to learn not to cross it.

Laurel

Dear Mom,

Words could never explain the love I have for you. For all my life I've wanted to tell you what an inspiration you are to me, but simple words like these could never begin to explain the way you fill my heart with love and hope each day. For almost fifteen years, you have given up so much of your life to dedicate your entire existence to me. You taught me so many things about school, sports, life, love, and myself, that I feel I will be in debt to you forever. I can't think of a time when you haven't been around to help me. You taught me to read when I was little. You played catch with me when I couldn't handle a ball. You came to all of my games and taught me how to shoot a lay-up. I know that I have been difficult at times and afraid to try new things, but you encouraged me to get involved and supported me in everything I wanted to do. You drove to dance classes and softball practices, took me to volleyball and basketball camps, kept me practicing my piano lessons even though I'd rather be outside. Remember when you were the cookie mom for my girl scout troop? These are only a few examples of the things you have done to share your never-ending love with me. You weren't only there for me physically, but emotionally as well. You've always stopped the tears when something was devastating me. You could always build up my confidence when I was feeling upset, inferior, or inadequate. I want to be everything you hope for me to be. I always want you to be proud of me and happy to tell others "That's my daughter!". Mom, you are my best friend. I can't think of anyone else who has been more important in my life. I love you very much and I am very proud to be your daughter.

Love,

Lisa

Dear mother,

Could you tell me what the word "LIFE" means to you? Unfortunately, it no longer means anything to me. Despair has taken hold of me.

We have never spent time together to just talk about whatever. I feel like I am really missing out on something! I've never heard you say what you really think of me. I don't know how I should feel, as a son, since you have never told me. When I have problems or I need help, you don't seem to be there. You seem distant to me. The little words of advice that a mother is supposed to pass on to her children, you must have forgotten them, since I've never seen any sign of them.

Extreme shyness seems to run in our family, it left its mark on me, and I suffer terribly because of it. It's very hard for me to make friends. I think about this problem all the time. I wish I could just express myself as I see fit.

What can I do? I don't know which way to turn any more. You give me the impression of being there only to blame me rather than give me any credit. What misery! What can I do except write this letter to make you understand how unhappy I am and how uncomfortable I am with myself. My dearest dream is to be part of a really tight-knit family, like five fingers on a hand, where we could tell each other the truth without being afraid of each other. But that seems to be nothing but a dream.

Mom, help me to find meaning in my life, before it's too late.

Your son who loves you,

Mark

Dear mom and dad,

I guess this would fall under the category of an apology, and I do believe you deserve one, but I am not going to apologize for what I said. I am apologizing for the way I said it. You always say that it isn't what you say, but the tone of voice you use, but I think the tone of voice I used was fully appropriate. I am apologizing for the words I used. I love you both very much, but it is true when I say that you are not the most open-minded people I know. I am not going to defend my friends from you, when you have never really met them and decide to make snap judgments about their character. My friends are not flawless, I will admit to that, but neither are you, and, in my opinion, I think you should put a higher emphasis on judging yourselves and making yourselves better people, than passing judgments on people you don't even know. I have realized that you don't even like your friends, that you think they are fake, shallow, and haughty, but they are "pretty" people, who are "normal".

I have friends who maybe don't look the way you would like them to look, but after that first impression they are real. They aren't the stereotype of their exterior, they are real people. I called you those names because I was angry, and I had all the right in the world to be angry. I just had no right to call you the names that I did. I am sorry for that. It is easy to drop to the level I dropped down to, and it's easy to throw names around, but it is not easy to listen to your parents put down people who you love. I am lucky to have friends that I like and who like me. In high school, real friends are hard to find. I found them... now you have to accept that and accept them for who they are.

I love you,

Talia

Dear Mommy,

I just wrote this letter because I wanted to express my feelings towards you and tell you how much I love you.

Sometimes, when we go through our little mother-daughter arguments/disagreements, I tend to say things that I really don't mean to say, but it just happens to come out. I have to admit that after all the arguments we have, I always ask God for his forgiveness. And everybody knows, including me, that God is not going to forgive anybody but so many times.

All I want to say is that I appreciate all that you have done for me to this day. What I love about you is that whenever I need something and you can't get it for me right then and there, then you will try your best to get it for me as soon as possible. That is why, hopefully, when I graduate from college and get a good job, I'm going to support you just as well as you supported me with beautiful things. Last but not least, my thanks for giving me life.

I love you,

Your middle daughter,

Shaeaye

PS: I know you don't want it to happen so fast but I am growing up, so therefore I just need a little more space.

Dear Mom and Dad,

How do I tell you how much I'm suffering? I never asked to be born. On the contrary, I would rather have never existed. What is the point of living if you don't exist for anybody? What is the point of living if your one and only wish is to disappear? The world is so cruel. Nobody understands me. Everyone judges me, a teenager struggling with drug problems, personality problems, and especially love problems. In the end, all I'm asking for is to be loved and accepted. It hurts so much to live that I no longer even dare close my eyes: I'm too afraid of being overcome by dark thoughts. Sometimes I want to scream out my anguish and tell off the society that's made me so rebellious and miserable. I'm really scared of growing up in this world without scruples, where horrific crimes are committed by young children. It's terrifying how society is falling apart through the influence of kids today. If we don't do something soon, life on earth will turn to dust, because there won't be a soul left. Is this what we want? It's up to us to decide.

evan

Dear Dad,

This is from your son Richie. You left when I was born, you never called, you never visited me!!! You missed my first step, you missed **15** of my birthdays and now you think, on my 16th birthday, you can just sleaze your way back into my life. I don't think so!!! Nothing that you do or will do would make me forgive you!!!

Not sincerely,

Your son,

Dear parents,

I know that not so long ago things weren't going very well between us. But when I noticed that you were making efforts to improve the situation, I felt really encouraged. I then wanted to make the necessary effort to work together and fix things between us. This way our family home could become what I've always wanted: a peaceful refuge, instead of a battlefield.

After thinking about what I could do for a long time, I figured out many things and made several resolutions. I'd like to share them with you.

I quickly figured out that by being vindictive, I would only succeed in hurting myself. I didn't want to hold a grudge against you, because I know that you, too, are far from being perfect, and that you make a lot of sacrifices for me. I know that when you impose certain things, which sometimes disappoint me, it's only because you love me and want the best for me. Luckily, you aren't one of those difficult or negligent parents. You are interested in me, and your interest isn't superficial. Plus, you try to set a good example. And believe it or not, I feel very privileged to have parents as good as you.

Most times I reject your instructions and don't accept your advice, only to realize later that you were right from start to finish. Why can't I learn to take advice? Don't worry, I will try to improve! I don't want a gulf to grow between us, a huge, irreparable rift. I don't want to become like all those other teens who admit to trying to spend as much time as possible away from home. I don't think that's a fun or ideal home situation.

I know you're older than me, and that you see life from a different angle. For example, we don't always have the same opinions concerning hairstyles, clothing or curfews. Being parents, you know that not everything in life turns out well. Certain bitter experiences in your childhood lessened the idealism of your youth. That, combined with the fact that you are older, probably explains why you don't always share my enthusiasm for some things. But none of this should prevent us from having fun together, whenever the occasion presents itself. Otherwise, we'd be letting it keep us from having a good relationship.

I'm perfectly aware that sometimes I do things I should have avoided. I find it very understandable that you are often sad or disappointed because of my actions. When I don't listen to your warnings, I shouldn't be surprised or mad if I'm greeted with a barrage of angry words. I deserved it.

I'll admit that if I want you to understand me, I must also make the effort to understand you. I agree that I need to be interested in you and concerned about your reasons for feeling such and such emotion, or reacting in a certain way. I shouldn't be so quick to judge you or to call you insensitive during family conflicts. At the same time, I shouldn't feel that your concern for me borders on paranoia. My reactions to your demands will have a big influence on the way you treat me. So, if we talked honestly from the start, surely we'd be able to avoid many misunderstandings. I promise I'll also do my bit to avoid conflict by trying to find solutions on my own, instead of rushing into things whenever something goes wrong.

I'm telling you all of this, but I'm omitting something: Mom and Dad, I love you more than anything in the world, and that's why I must tell you more.

I know that what you taught me when I was little was for my own good because you knew that, sooner or later in my life, I would need that knowledge. For example, when you taught me to put away my toys, it was so that later I'd realize the importance of tidying my room and cleaning my future house. When you taught me the alphabet, it was to interest me in intellectual pursuits at a young age, so I could appreciate them and take part in them in the future. This no doubt explains why I've done so well in school, from elementary school up to now. Other things help me think about and accept discipline for even the smallest things. For example, when you ask me to run an errand, I don't always want to. But then I think of all the time you spent teaching me to walk, and how useful that is to me, and I'm very grateful. When something makes me sad, I remember that it was you who taught me to smile. Just thinking about it makes me smile and my sadness disappears.

When you ask me to spend some time helping you, I think of all the hours you spent teaching me the basic things in life. I know that the smallest things made you happy because you felt like you'd accomplished something. I can't imagine how pleased you must have been when I smiled for the first time, ate using a spoon on my own, said my first words, or took my first steps on my own. I know that, to this day, when I accomplish something good, you are proud of yourselves, because it's thanks to you, and proud of me, because I'm your daughter. In several years, when you will become older, I will continue to honor and respect you out of gratitude for everything you've done for me. I will be very pleased to do everything I can for you, and because of that, you will always have a high opinion of me.

Mom and Dad, I promise I will change. I will try to improve our family life. The peaceful relations we will have from now on will make up for all the time I wasted fighting with you. But I'm not perfect, and neither you nor I can perform miracles. So, if I sometimes slack off, please understand and let me know, so I can get right back on track.

But you too, dear parents, must remember this: I don't know what words to use to tell you how glad I am that you are my parents and how much I love you.

And I won't lose sight of my greatest resolution: proving all this to you.

Mom and Dad, I LOVE YOU.

Sincerely,
Your daughter,

Leslie

Expressing ourselves is often easier in writing than verbally. We have reserved this space for you, for your words. Let your pen caress these pages

with liberty, free of judgement. If your unveiling carries you to the limits of the paper, don't hesitate to attach other sheets inside the book!

Dear parents,

As you know, I am not really very
demonstrative and I have trouble
showing my feelings, so I decided
to take a few moments of my time
to write this letter to you.

These days, the life of a teenage boy or
girl is not always easy. We begin our lives
with all the problems it entails. I know it's hard for you, but
try to remember when you were our age; I'm sure you took
advantage of it like all the other kids. I know that I am difficult
to live with, because, let's face it, my temper leaves something
to be desired. When there is some little snag in my life, I often
take it out on you, but that is not because I don't love you.
On the contrary, I love you both, even you dad, who are no
longer with us. When I get mad, I know I say nasty things, but
I don't necessarily mean what I say. I would need to control
myself more and learn to communicate with you, mom, because
when I have a heavy heart, I keep it to myself, and after a
while I explode in anger. I made you a promise, Dad, and I'm
going to keep it. You can be sure of that. These days I know
it's difficult for everybody, but I find that I have changed. I
mind my own business more, Mom, and argue a lot less with
my sister than I used to. I am proud of that!

I am very sad that you are gone, dad. I regret so much the
last few months when I had something important to tell you.
But now I am taking advantage of this special opportunity to
say it to you, because I know you can see me and you are
listening. I want to tell you again that I love you with all my
heart and I was not always nice to you; I am sorry for that. I
wish I had paid more attention to you when you told me about
life, but what you said troubled me, and that's why today I feel

stupid to have acted like that. I thank you for everything you do for me, because I know you still watch over us and protect us like you always did.

I want to talk about my freedom. For a sixteen-year-old girl, I am not allowed to do very much. Yet you have changed since last year, mom, and I do feel less tied down. As you know, Mary is two years younger than me, and she can do pretty much what she wants; while I have trouble getting your permission to spend an evening with friends if there's smoking and drinking going on. I know that you are concerned about me and you want me to be healthy, but if my friends smoke it doesn't mean I have to follow their example! On the other hand, a beer or two won't kill me, and anyway I can control myself. I want you to remember that I'm sixteen and I am responsible for myself. Remember, at fourteen I did not have the freedom that my sister has now. I need to live my life as I see fit, and freedom is very impor-tant for a girl my age. I am sure you understand that.

All these pages to tell you what I can't say to you in person. Maybe I've lacked the courage to talk to you, but now you know what I think. I hope you're not angry about things I wrote in this letter, but you had to find them out sooner or later.

Your daughter who loves you and cares for you very much,

Sheryl

Dear Mother and Father,

Your lamb... you have hurt him. You will break him, you will kill him, before he even decides to bleat out his pain. The sheep rages against those who paint him black, but his rebellion doesn't make him any less of a sheep. So he holds back anger on the edge of his lips and swallows his cynicism.

His heart plots against him along with you, the judges: his infinite magnanimity and extreme kindness give you absolute power. Your false looks enclose him in petty judgments as in an open jail. You don't understand. You don't know. You never question anything; you choke on your own certainties that taste of bitter ashes. All those who don't share your dull thoughts are worthless. You rely on an impregnable reason. The sheep rejects your reason. It doesn't give him anything that's worth living for. It confines him in small truths that are dull and insignificant.

You love poorly. You've never been taught how, and you've passed on your ignorance like a cursed legacy to your sheep, but this doesn't seem to matter to you. You have withered your heart with all your reasoning. Too bad for the sheep whose heart is even bigger than his reason... You have chloroformed your dreams in order to believe in your

routine happiness. You close yourselves like a clam when some calling into question might open your eyes. You mock the sheep's seriousness, you laugh at his questions, you deplore his outbursts of anger with condescending pity and a vague uneasiness. You are then surprised by his anger, but push

away the reasons for it with a sweep of the hand. The reasons of the heart are of no consequence to people of your experience. An incurable disease consumes them. They suffer from acute respectable "adultitis" in its terminal stage.

You don't understand the idealistic quest for absolutes of the sheep, his hunger for the Little Prince's essential violent rose, his sensitivity full of emotions, teetering at the abyss. Yet the sheep's blackness is incumbent upon you; instead of daylight, you have given him the night. Your cup of gall and venom provokes his idiotic silence close to madness. Since you can't read in the infinite anger of a scared sheep all his desperate love for the world, then bear being informed of the cause of his rebellion. He hurts from loving you so profoundly.

Your lamb lost in this world of wolves,

Miles

Mom,

I will remember that day for the rest of my life. When I got home from school, you sat me down. I was afraid of the look in your eyes. You started talking, but all your words sounded wrong in my head. A month ago, you found a lump in one of your breasts. After several examinations, your doctor told you it was benign. But still, what a shock! Your doctor had you go through more tests, just to be sure. I remember that one of my old friends lost her mother after they discovered one of those damn lumps! I don't want to lose you. Maybe some people will say I'm crazy to worry about a little lump that's benign anyway, but for me that lump represents my future with you, Mom. You're only 36 and I'm only 15. We still have so many things to do together. Maybe you won't leave for the hereafter today, but I know that one day it will happen. And I'm not ready for that. In any case, I don't think I'll ever be ready. Mom, I want you to be at my wedding, to be there when your grandchildren are born, to share our joys and our sorrows.

What I want to say to young and old alike is that our parents are important. We mustn't waste a second with them. Don't wake up only after they're gone, because it will be too late, and then you'll regret it for the rest of your life. For me, from that day on, I realized that my mother would leave one day. Before that, it hadn't really sunk in. After all, our parents will always be there for us, right? Well, I can say this isn't true. They won't ALWAYS be there, because the dead can't help the living. So don't miss your opportunity. Don't wait until your parents are no longer around to make your peace with them. Embrace your life together! And above all, take care of them. Me, I love my mother. Sure, we still have little arguments; it's just that life is too short to get caught up in those fights. Life is meant to be lived, not spoiled.

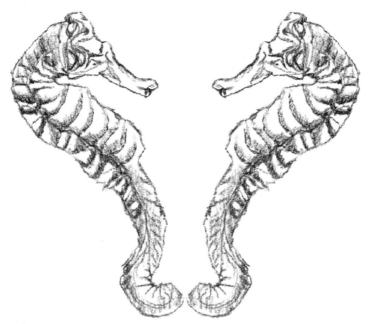

Dear Dad,

This past week, I've been
really thinking about our father and daughter relationship. It's
funny, it's been sixteen years that I've been your daughter and
we've had our good and bad moments but the words "I love
you" have never been uttered. I know it's really hard for you to
express your emotions, but maybe you could show me that you
love me and appreciate me in another way. Everything I do is
done with the hope that I'll please you. It's difficult for a child
to please her parent when he doesn't give a sign of encou-
ragement. I know it's going to hurt if you read this letter, but it
also hurts me a lot, so much so that I've cried a river of tears
thinking about this. Everything would be okay if I could hear you
say, those three simple words, "I love you.", just once.

With lots of love,

From your beloved daughter,

Caufa

Dear Mom,
Dear Dad,

It's me, your daughter, talking to you. Oh, I know you have trouble recognizing me, seeing your daughter in me. But I also have trouble recognizing myself. I feel like my body is growing and my soul is trying to grow as well but it can't seem to keep up. You know, growing up is painful. I see everyone around me through a wall of ice. Sunbeams shine on the wall but they can't make it melt. Images of you are distant and distorted. I feel cut off from you. I'd like to take an ice pick and shatter this wall of misunderstanding. Have you forgotten what it's like to be a teenager? To try to find yourself? To want to jump headfirst into life, all the while feeling an indescribable fear of the future? I feel as strong as a lioness and as weak as a kitten.

Stop asking me if I'm feeling okay when I shut myself in my room. The answer is yes, I'm fine. I just need to be alone, to organize things in my head, to sort out the feelings in my heart. When too many of my feelings get tangled together, I feel lost. I don't know myself anymore. It's very difficult to untangle these knots in my heart in this "wonderful" period called adolescence.

Don't worry. I love life and I'm not thinking of precipitating my departure towards the Great Beyond. It's just that... I don't really know what provokes this melancholy. Is it something that happens automatically with adolescence? I don't think so, because I've seen teenagers who smile and seem happy. I don't mean to say that I'm always in a bad mood, it's just that I feel numb. Yes, numb, that's the word. I'm not worried about all this, though. One day, I'll pull myself together, and get out of this state. In the mean time, let me be happy as a "zombie".

That's what I wanted to say to you. Maybe this letter doesn't make any sense to you, but remember that it comes from the bottom of my heart. There's only one more thing I want to say, the most important one: I love you.

Helen

Dearest Mom, dearest Dad,

As you already know, my best friend's mother died two years ago. Ever since her death, Sara's life has been completely different from mine. She has tons of responsibilities: she cooks for her family of three, does the laundry and cleans the house.

I'm writing to you because I don't think I do you justice. I'll admit that I'm difficult to handle. I get mad when I can't talk on the phone, when you enforce my curfew, when I have to take the dog out for a walk, and when I have to pick up my room. These kinds of things really get to me, but I know you discipline me so I'll be well brought up. I appreciate you at your true value. I think of Sara often, playing the role of mother in her family. I know I'm lucky to have such great parents who love me dearly and are always there for me. Sara doesn't get to hang out with our gang very often now because she's too busy. Now, I realize how much freedom I really have.

Mom, Dad, I'm so sorry we've had so many fights in the past. Since the death of Sara's mother, I've realized how much we don't appreciate what we've got until it's gone. I want you to know I am very grateful for all you do for me, and I'm really glad I enjoy a happy life. I owe that to you.

Kind regards,

Cynthia

Dear Mom and Dad,

So many ideas, so much joy, so much anger, jumbled up inside me. Today I want to turn them loose. Sometimes a little door in my heart opens and tries to attract your attention, but it usually fails. I wish I was able to talk about what I feel, struggling with my daily problems. I wish I could express my feelings to you and not be ashamed of crying in front of you. I try to talk to you sometimes, but my lips hesitate, they can't do it.

I get the impression that you've forgotten that part of your lives called adolescence, and that you don't want to remember it. This period of life brings with it many changes, both physical and psychological. I feel I'm getting lost in the process. Hidden under my covers, I sometimes cry, thinking about our numerous daily arguments. I often regret my words, but I never have the guts to tell you. I also shed tears over thoughtless things you've said to me. Most of the time, I know you don't really mean them, but just hearing them hurts me a lot. Instead of fighting, couldn't we spend more time telling each other that we love each other?

Ever since I was little, I've always been nervous and worried about everything. I don't want to put all the blame on you, Mom, but I think you have something to do with it. I'd really like to feel more comfortable at home. I'd like to get along better with both of you, but especially you, Mom.

I hope this letter will improve our relationships because in spite of how it may seem, I love you both very very much.

Andrew

Dear Mom,

I've recently decided to write you a letter but I doubt you will receive it anytime soon. Life has been so hard for me lately. School, guys, and life have really been depressing me. However, I usually manage to get by. I really miss you being there for me. Ever since the divorce, years back, I have this feeling of being cheated. You're never there for me when the important things in my life go on. You don't even act like a mother to me. Then when I go to you for help or just a person to talk to, you start to compare our problems. It's not my fault you're unhappy with your boyfriend but evidently he was chosen by you and chosen over me. Your absence in my life has left me to depend on my father who is more to me than anything in the world. It has also left me this hatred towards you. When I get older I will still have these feelings of alienation towards you. I probably won't even decide to marry or have children because of this belief that marriage always ends in divorce. In addition, my feelings for my family have diminished. Since you and my dad dislike each other, I am tortured with the fact that I will never be close with an extended family. It is a dream to me, to be able to have a family where everyone is there.

Anyhow thanks for my childhood memories and for making efforts when possible. I just wish you weren't such a lame duck. Maybe one day you will come around but one day it just might be too late. The choice is yours.

Sincerely,

Luisa

PS: I'll always love you, regardless of your mistakes.

Dear Mom,

Sometimes when I lie awake at night, I think about some of the things that have changed since I was a kid. Some things really bother me. I can't remember when I last kissed you good night and told you that "I love you." I remember when I was a child, I wouldn't go to sleep until you came to tuck me in and I don't know when or why this all stopped.

When I was young, you'd tell me how quickly I was growing and here I am, I just turned sixteen years old. I have many years ahead of me but where did those sixteen years go?

To me, time is the most powerful thing that exists. No one has any control over it. There is nothing I can do to stop it or slow it down. What I can do is take advantage of the time we have. I hope you know I'm thankful for every moment we spend together, even though I don't always show it.

I love you,

Anne

Dear Dad, dear Mom,

I'm writing this letter to you to express my love and gratitude. You know how hard it is for me to say how I feel! I think I'll find it easier to write.

Yes, I love you! You mean more to me than anyone else. I realize this now, at the dawn of my sixteenth birthday. I've sorted through all my memories, but I can't think of a single day when you didn't show me your love. Whether it was a soothing word, a loving glance, or a friendly hug, you have always been there for me, to comfort me, encourage me or congratulate me. You have given me so much, have shared so much with me! Among other things, you showed me how to see the bright side of life, and to never get discouraged because God is there watching over me.

I must admit that for many years I didn't believe in your "God stories." But you persisted; you introduced me to people who believed in Him and were happy. I think that was the detail that, little by little, changed my way of seeing things. These people had a light in their eyes, a smile on their lips, confidence in their hearts and their faces were serene. They shared with me their life stories, their experiences, their way of living. They showed me a loving, faithful, friendly God.

By overcoming adversity, I learned. With your love and the love of all those around me, I have grown. A sincere faith was born in my heart. Thanks to you, I too am happy, confident and serene. I cannot thank you enough for this precious gift. Happiness is the greatest gift of all!

Your daughter who loves you more and more each day,

Laurie

Dear Mom,

The purpose of this letter is I want you know that I really feel comfortable now talking to you. At first, it was really hard to let you know everything I was going through (especially with the guys). But now, I can speak to you as if you were one of my friends. Now, I can really talk to you whenever I may run into any difficult problems in life. Whenever I am confused about anything, I can always come and speak to you. And after I speak to you, I feel all the better because I know that you've gone through the same problems. With experience, you'll be able to help me straighten things out. Not all daughters can speak to their mother the way I can speak to you. This is why I want you to really know how much I appreciate you for being my mother.

Sincerely yours,

Janya

Dear parents,

I doubt that this letter will ever be given to you. It's difficult enough for me to write what I would so much like to tell you, so how can I hope to have the courage to give you written that which I cannot express to you face-to-face. Nevertheless, I am writing it, in hopes that it can be useful one day...

Sometimes life is wonderful; sometimes it is sad. This is my analysis of life, looking back over my sixteen years. Whether it's so beautiful it brings tears or so sad one can't bear it, I need to talk about it, to confide in someone.

There are times when I'm in such a state of euphoria that it's impossible not to share my joy with the entire world. The first people I want to talk to about my happiness are the two of you. But too often, I feel that what I say doesn't interest you, or that you just aren't listening to me at all!

Maybe it does interest you, but you don't show it. And then you accuse me of not talking, of keeping everything to myself. Before making such accusations, maybe it would be worthwhile to stop working for a moment and analyze your own behavior when I try to communicate something to you.

It also seems to me that I get a lot more attention and lectures for doing the wrong thing than praise for doing the right thing.

It seems you look at me as if I were a Van Gogh painting and only see the minuscule spot that no one else notices.

I would also like to tell you that contrary to what most adults think, it's not easy to be a teenager. Among the difficulties that I experience in my life is school.

At the beginning of the year, I arrive at school willing and full of good intentions. Then, as the year goes by, my willingness and good intentions run out. At the beginning of the year, I studied for my tests a week ahead, then a few days ahead, then the night before... But now with the school year almost over, even the night before an important exam, I can't find the will, I can't find the energy to study any more. It's like I'm tired of everything having to do with school. I go to school for one thing only: to have as much fun as possible with the ones who cheer me up when I'm down: my friends.

Anyone who might read this will think I have bad parents. But they would be wrong because I have the greatest parents in the world. Despite these misunderstandings that come between us, I think that I can count myself lucky to have you as parents.

Your son,

Martin

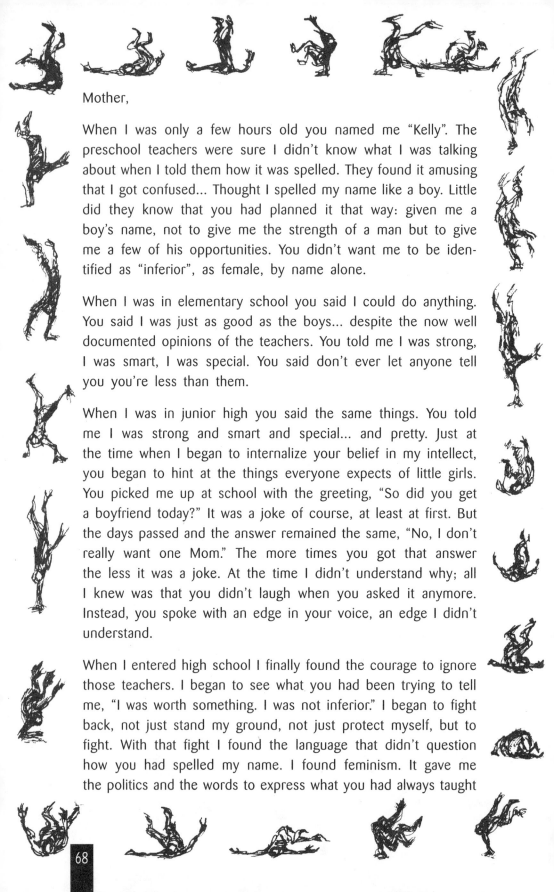

Mother,

When I was only a few hours old you named me "Kelly". The preschool teachers were sure I didn't know what I was talking about when I told them how it was spelled. They found it amusing that I got confused... Thought I spelled my name like a boy. Little did they know that you had planned it that way: given me a boy's name, not to give me the strength of a man but to give me a few of his opportunities. You didn't want me to be identified as "inferior", as female, by name alone.

When I was in elementary school you said I could do anything. You said I was just as good as the boys... despite the now well documented opinions of the teachers. You told me I was strong, I was smart, I was special. You said don't ever let anyone tell you you're less than them.

When I was in junior high you said the same things. You told me I was strong and smart and special... and pretty. Just at the time when I began to internalize your belief in my intellect, you began to hint at the things everyone expects of little girls. You picked me up at school with the greeting, "So did you get a boyfriend today?" It was a joke of course, at least at first. But the days passed and the answer remained the same, "No, I don't really want one Mom." The more times you got that answer the less it was a joke. At the time I didn't understand why; all I knew was that you didn't laugh when you asked it anymore. Instead, you spoke with an edge in your voice, an edge I didn't understand.

When I entered high school I finally found the courage to ignore those teachers. I began to see what you had been trying to tell me, "I was worth something. I was not inferior." I began to fight back, not just stand my ground, not just protect myself, but to fight. With that fight I found the language that didn't question how you had spelled my name. I found feminism. It gave me the politics and the words to express what you had always taught

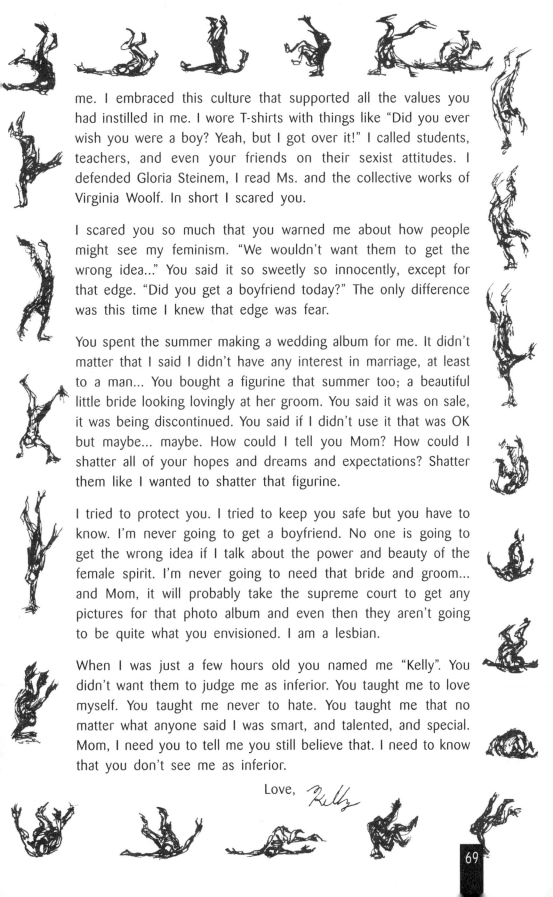

me. I embraced this culture that supported all the values you had instilled in me. I wore T-shirts with things like "Did you ever wish you were a boy? Yeah, but I got over it!" I called students, teachers, and even your friends on their sexist attitudes. I defended Gloria Steinem, I read Ms. and the collective works of Virginia Woolf. In short I scared you.

I scared you so much that you warned me about how people might see my feminism. "We wouldn't want them to get the wrong idea..." You said it so sweetly so innocently, except for that edge. "Did you get a boyfriend today?" The only difference was this time I knew that edge was fear.

You spent the summer making a wedding album for me. It didn't matter that I said I didn't have any interest in marriage, at least to a man... You bought a figurine that summer too; a beautiful little bride looking lovingly at her groom. You said it was on sale, it was being discontinued. You said if I didn't use it that was OK but maybe... maybe. How could I tell you Mom? How could I shatter all of your hopes and dreams and expectations? Shatter them like I wanted to shatter that figurine.

I tried to protect you. I tried to keep you safe but you have to know. I'm never going to get a boyfriend. No one is going to get the wrong idea if I talk about the power and beauty of the female spirit. I'm never going to need that bride and groom... and Mom, it will probably take the supreme court to get any pictures for that photo album and even then they aren't going to be quite what you envisioned. I am a lesbian.

When I was just a few hours old you named me "Kelly". You didn't want them to judge me as inferior. You taught me to love myself. You taught me never to hate. You taught me that no matter what anyone said I was smart, and talented, and special. Mom, I need you to tell me you still believe that. I need to know that you don't see me as inferior.

Love, Kelly

Dearest mom,

You have always been a source of inspiration and happiness for me, and the love you show me provides me with a sense of security. I know I don't always follow the path you would like me to take. I see how much you want to protect me from life's pitfalls while hoping I will make the right choices. The fact that you are proud of me fills me with joy, and when, unfortunately, I disappoint you, I suffer with you. From your love and your experience, I have learned everything that has made me who I am and that gives me the strength to believe in myself. You showed me how to recognize in myself the ability to achieve my full potential. Perhaps I don't always choose the easiest path, and I may sometimes be wrong, but I've learned to make my own decisions based on what I believe is right at that moment, knowing full well that my decision might change with time.

Although it's not always easy for you to understand my actions, don't forget, mother dearest, that from the depths of my being, you have, and you will always have, a special place in my heart. No matter what paths I choose, I will always respect your judgment, even if I don't always accept it as my own.

I love you, mom, and I can only hope to give others as much of myself as you have given of yourself to me.

Your daughter who admires you and loves you very much,

Naomi

Mother,

My eyes, ringed with the pain of living, worry you. You didn't dare question me. I didn't dare answer...

Most teens swear by "the present." Me, I hate it. Nothing and no one is there for me. To endure it, to survive without reason towards a future that doesn't seem much better. I'm left only with the past to hang onto.

I remember innocence. I remember another: me.

But too soon, my mind went into a downward spin, chewing over my life (because at that time I was living), and started to question itself. I realized, among other things, who I am. Nothing is worse than discovering who we really are. I've barely begun, the worst has yet to come.

Some will call me a coward. They will accuse me of running away, of hiding in my memories. They will tell me I need to face life. Well, they will be delighted to hear that someone has recently soiled the symbol of my dear past. From now on, I am confronted by a merciless present.

Deprived of my childhood, I tried to live, but I couldn't bear the suffering anymore.

Behind a mask, I'm now letting another confront my life.

I thought I had the answer when I figured out that everything has a price. Ephemeral masks merge in you and distort you. You hurriedly put on another one, then another, then another... Disappointed with who you've become, those around you abandon you, one by one.

Alone, with a me that is no longer me, I sink, while others move forward.

Do you understand, Mom? Explain it to me because I'm lost. Am I really, or do I just want to be?

Kate

Dear Daddy,

Today, I decided to write to you because I haven't written in over a year already. I'm also writing to tell you how much I miss you and how hard your leaving was for me. It's been over a year now since you died from brain cancer. Of course, we did live through your two years of illness before that, and we were able to go through a lot of our feelings together. But I must admit those two years were as hard as the year I just spent without you, if not harder. That's why I wanted to write you this letter and tell you about my fears and my emotions - both past and present, and probably future as well.

For starters, I'd like to tell you what seemed the hardest to bear among all the burdens and consequences of your cancer. I found it especially hard to see you getting constantly weaker, since before you usually could do anything. You know, it was very hard for me to see you become more and more powerless, to see how excruciatingly hard it was for you to even get up from your chair. I wanted so much to tell you it was okay to be slower, but I could see that slowing down reduced your ability to do things by half. It was also hard for me to treat you like a child, having to tell you not to do things because the effort exhausted you. I really didn't enjoy playing the role of parent with you. It's one thing with a doll, but with my father... I must say I wouldn't want to do it again. In fact, I think what disturbed me the most in those situations was glimpsing all the sadness in your eyes. I thought I could see a world full of dreams in your eyes, dreams you were no longer entitled to because of your illness.

Sometimes, I remember certain things we did all together as a family, and then... I start to cry. The worst part is

I'm not sure why. I don't know anymore if my tears are tears of sadness or tears of joy. Sadness because we will never again be all together to do whatever I'm thinking about, or joy because I'm remembering the "good old days" and the happiness we felt then.

Another thing that drew many tears was the hospital. The famous hospital of no return. "No return" because once you went there, you never came back. Each time I visited you in the hospital, I felt lucky I could leave and go outside. Whenever I saw the tiny window through which you could glimpse a little bit of greenery, I imagined myself tearing down the hospital and building another one with windows that were ten times bigger.

Some people who came to see you seemed like executioners or enemies to me (the nurses, for example...) I think my reaction was normal. I hated when the nurses gave you needles or stole some of the time we had to see you. I was almost jealous of your friends, as if they too stole time away from me.

Some days, I think about what you must have gone through during your illness. I can see that the roles of cancer patient and "patient companion" are different. What affected me the most in all this, is the loss, the emptiness. I thought I was the saddest person in the world, because I was losing my dad. But one day, I suddenly realized: "I can say I've lost my father, but my father has lost his family, his friends, his work, his hobbies, and even his dreams." If love makes you blind, sadness does too, because you'd think I would have figured that out sooner! Once I did, I felt like I'd been too preoccupied with my own little self. This bugged me, so naturally, I changed my outlook. From then on, I didn't feel as sad and I finally realized how strong you had been to be able to bear losing everything you had. If I'd been in your shoes, I don't think I would have been able to keep smiling, as you did, until your last breath.

I went through many stages before accepting, partly, your death. Among other things, I was very scared during the inevitable denial stage. In fact, that's when I started to think Jesus was a fake, that he'd only been an idiot-savant who just thought he was the son of God. And just to show you how much I was doubting Jesus, I figured out technically how he'd performed all his miracles, including walking on water. But before denigrating Jesus completely, I asked Mom to help me regain my faith. She managed by telling me that it's not Jesus' miracles or actions that are important, so much as what we've learned from them. Thankfully, that put an end to my doubting. (I wanted to tell you this story to show you how I over-came my denial of your approaching death. Compared with me, that stage must have been especially hard for you, eh?)

I'd like to tell you what death represents for me now. At first, death seemed like a loss and an infinite sadness to me. After crying a seemingly endless amount of tears, I saw death from a very different perspective, very dif-ferent. For the first time, I saw something positive in death, since I noticed that I had changed. I am now able to see the bright side in every situation. Of course, I didn't develop a positive attitude overnight. I managed though, and I'm proud of myself because it's really thanks to you. Little by little, I saw death as a rebirth of the self. Just like the seedling cut from the spider plant to make a new plant, I took what I had left of you and used it to rebuild my life more solidly. I must admit my adolescence was greatly shaken by your death. But now, thanks to you, death has become something beautiful that I'm still trying to make more beautiful. I've learned to see the essential in life: not a big house, or a car, but rather being satisfied with the best our lives offer us. Like seeing a little bird on a branch. I know seeing a bird is not a big deal, but at moments like this, I realize that bird could have landed on another branch and the fact that he didn't is a gift my life has given me. For me, that's what is the Essential now. I've figured out a whole lot of other things like that, things I'd never realized before.

One of the last things I want to tell you is about my fears for the future. I'm so scared of forgetting your face, your voice, your laughter, the things you did, and the food you liked to eat. Or forgetting the way you held me in your arms. One day, I got scared you'd die and I'd have forgotten your last words to me. So from that day on until the end, I listened attentively to everything you said, remembering your last words. Then one day, instinctively I think, I knew your last word was coming so I etched it in my memory with the tone of voice you had when you said it. All this to say that my last visits to you were horrible, like the last time I left you and said "I love you, Daddy." Those are the moments I'm so scared of forgetting. Even though they seemed awful to me, I want to keep them inside me forever, like a legacy.

I'm scared, too, of missing the things we used to do together. Like watching hockey in your room, or travelling... Luckily, we were able to fulfill our common dream:

to travel together, just you and me. We were supposed to go to another country, but had to stay here, because of your illness. I want you to know I don't mind that much anymore that we didn't go very far, because I was with you and that was the main thing.

In the end, Daddy, I owe you my pride, my courage and my determination. Without you, I never would have experienced all the good things that have happened and will happen to me before I meet you again. I don't regret a second of those three years that went by so fast, as fast as a landscape flies by our eyes in a train. Because I know that had even one second or one action been changed in the course of my life, I wouldn't be here now, writing you this letter, writing you these words that were hidden deep inside me for too long.

I hope I'll have the time and the presence of mind to write to you again.

From your most beautiful daughter (as you used to call me, even though I was your only one),

Kimberly

Dear Mom and Dad,

I know lately I haven't been the best daughter.
I know I say things that are very cruel at
times, but I don't mean them. I say those
things because I'm angry, not at you, but
at other things that I myself have to deal
with. It's not fair that I take out my anger
on you, I'm so sorry.

Also, lately I have been ignoring you. I know
it hurts you, but those are not my intentions.
There are some problems I have that I have to
handle on my own, and I often push away others
whom I love. This has nothing to do with you,
so please understand.

You're my parents and I love you very much
and I would never do anything to hurt you. I
just need some time to figure things out for
myself. I just need you to understand and
cooperate with me. I love you.

Love,

Dear parents,

What is your idea of the perfect child? The one you secretly, shamefully dream of when your first offspring makes you see red? Without a doubt, the sublime, classic image of the model child dances in your head: lovable, polite, intelligent, well-behaved, obedient... . And surely you know someone who fits into this category. The daughter of one of your friends, for example. The girl whose image sneaks into your head despite yourself, when you run across some old rag that belongs to your own beloved teen. Oh, if only your own child was as wonderful as such a girl... . But tell me, what do you really know about this teen you dream of so? Think about it. Hmmm... hard to say, right? The fact is that you have no idea what she or he is really like as a person. All you know is the surface of their being. So now, dear parents, allow me to shed some light on the subject for you...

I am what you might call a model teen. I get good grades in school, I am polite and people consider me to be a serious and reasonable young woman. However, my mother would often gladly trade me for another and, if I were her, I'd do the same. Because unfortunately for my parents, although I'm exceptionally calm and well-mannered at school and in the homes of others, it's another story once I set foot in my own home. My personality drastically changes then. I grumble and get caustic and gloomy. The veneer I wear all day crumbles to reveal a less radiant side of me. The situation has reached the point where I almost can't stand myself. Elsewhere, I'm always willing to make myself useful, but at home, I often refuse to lift a little finger to help. Imagine: I'm sixteen and I can't even cook potatoes! Sometimes, I despise myself. I'm so dishonest! I'm two-faced as we say. But, what do you want, it's beyond me. I can't help conforming to the image people have of me and it's impossible for me to be pleasant with my family. I really don't know why, but maybe it's that I force myself so much to be good at school that when I get home it all explodes. Then I feel I'm loosing control over myself. Pretty discouraging, isn't it? Admit it, this is not how you imagined me at all!

That was on the family front.. Now let me tell you about my friends. Obviously I never have very many and it's rare for me to keep them very long. This is due to several factors. The most important is the personality clash between myself and other people. I rarely meet young people who really understand me. I think to them I am a mystery. Too complicated, paradoxical. I have probably only ever met one other person like me. Result: we can't stand each other. Pretty funny, right? It certainly gives one something to think about...

As you have no doubt noticed, I am not what you would call a happy girl. I know I'm brilliant, but it sets me apart from the others and people don't like those on the fringe. I came to realize this very much despite myself: during a period of my life I found extremely long, people ridiculed and rejected me, called me "Brainiac" because I did so well in class. It made me miserable for years. If you have never been through that, you can't understand it. I am not pretty, nor particularly funny or likable. The one thing I had going for me was my intelligence and they made fun of it. It drove me to tears! Today things have changed. Now I tell those who laugh at me where to go. With the risk of being cliché, I would say that I have built a shell to protect myself. I wouldn't go so far as to say that I avoid all human contact, but I do keep my distance.

I used to be very emotional. I still am, in my moments. But whether I like it or not, I always keep my cool. Sad to say, sometimes it seems to me I have no feelings. None. Total emptiness. Strange, isn't it? And sometimes, it's completely the opposite. I laugh, I cry over nothing and I run through the whole range of possible emotions. How would you react if you had such a bizarre child? I certainly have no idea how I would. I dare hope that if I ever have a kid, it won't take after me. Because that would be one manipulative child. I am ashamed to admit it, but that is one of my character traits. I "play" with people. I tell them what they want to hear to get them to think like me. I use various tactics and strategies to do it, and I almost always get what I want. Oh! I must seem awful to you!

I don't describe myself in flattering terms, I know. In my defense I can say that I nonetheless have my good points like anybody else. I won't make you sit through a countdown of them, even though it is a rather short list. You must know my positive side fairly well, since that is what I usually reveal. But despite the spitefulness that I can display, I have also had my share of misery. I've always had to conform to what people expected of me and I could never disappoint. My parents were always very strict with me. I was, and I still am, sewn up in a cocoon where I can't make my own decisions. It's very difficult to always be told what to do and say. And I must never come home from school with a grade under 90%, because what a scene that is! Even though my marks have always been excellent, my parents still ask me if I study enough! I am constantly observed, monitored. My father and mother don't trust me, even though I have never done anything reprehensible. Quite often I get a smothering feeling that won't go away, and makes me want to scream. If one day all my feelings blow, if all this frustration in me escapes, it won't be pretty! I dream of escaping the control of my parents, and if I decide... Here, I'm sending a message to all the parents of "good" children: do not underestimate the rage your child can feel. Sometimes it's the most well-behaved children that can surprise you...

So dear parents, do you see now what a sweet innocent face can hide? Do you understand that you should not trust a Cherub's smile? If so, I have achieved my goal: to demolish the myth of the model child. You must be somewhat disappointed. I have taken away your dream. But don't worry, model children aren't monsters; they are simply kids like any others... or almost. Consider yourself lucky to have the child you have. The grass is always greener on the other side of the fence. As for the model children, never trust appearances. Take it from a big brain!

Candice

Dear parents,

It's crazy how pride can stop the heart from speaking out. All those accusations and insults are so much easier to express than what I'd really like to say to you. I thank God that I have you in every one of my prayers.

Adolescence is the age of rebellion. Unfortunately, you're part of it very often. I get the impression that at a certain point in life, all adults are the same - serious and materialistic - and they no longer want to dream. But, on some other days, I look at you from a different angle, and I'm so proud that you're MY parents. In your thinking, your old-fashioned way, I can often recognize myself. I know you'd like to know everything about me: my joys, my sorrows, my mistakes, and all that I hide from you. Don't hold it against me, but even though I'm young, I value my private life. All the hurtful things I may have said to you hurt me as much as they hurt you. I think I will forever live to regret my words. I owe much of my happiness to you. Whatever may happen, my love for you is growing every day. Today, maybe for the first time, I'm saying "I love you." Not "I love you," casually, as you might say to anyone, but "I love you" most sincerely, from a daughter to the people she loves the most in the world.

Jennifer

In this place is a tale of a letter that didn't make the book...

Not all goes smoothly putting a project such as this together. Each of our authors was asked to sign and return a contract, both for legal purposes, and to demonstrate their seriousness and commitment to the book. The contract for this letter never was returned, making it impossible to include it here.

The young male author sent back the contract but it got lost in the mail. Since the deadline was approaching, we faxed a second copy to him at his high school. The day it arrived, he got into trouble. He was being admonished by the principal at the moment the contract was handed to him by a teacher, in the principal's office. The principal said that, in his opinion, the teen didn't deserve to represent the school since he was such a bad student, failing his classes, etc. etc. etc. We do not know what exact trouble he was in, except for his falling grades. The young author didn't send the contract back, even when Sonia Bahl, the president of our publishing house, told him that he didn't represent his school, that this book wasn't about schools but about teenagers expressing themselves freely.

The last time Sonia talked to him on the phone, she told him that in her opinion, even if he were a problem child, failing his classes, being a pest, he had the right to his opinions, his emotions. He wasn't unintelligent or insensitive. His letter touched her and many test readers. Ironically, he admitted in his letter that he did often disobey orders. He was trying to explain why he behaved that way, and making amends for it. Sonia wondered if the principal ever read his letter.

We are sorry we can't share it with you.

Dear Mom and Dad, out of love I write to you...

There are days when you want to shout to your dear ones: "I love you!" the way you might say it to your boyfriend or girlfriend. But then there are days when you want to say "I love you" in a different way like "I love you Dad. I love you, Mom... "

Growing from the cradle I was once in, now I'm in my own clothes, extravagant, large, tight, or little girl style. Today, dear parents, I have become a young woman, maybe not always up to scratch, but who tries to show who she is wherever she is. I know, I'm sometimes difficult to live with, I do have my grumpy side, but that doesn't stop me from appreciating you anyway.

As the little singer in the house, with my jumping around, my squealing, my imitations and my erratic movements, forgive me for my wild youth, but you know me, I'm as unpredictable as a chameleon. I admit I'm always worked up and excited. I must drive you crazy! And you put up with me so patiently! I'm a spinning top, happy to whirl around amid such a great family. I'm lucky to become a woman surrounded by your understanding and your love.

Dad, Mom, you know that during adolescence it's sometimes hard to express feelings in words, but when I write, I find it so much easier. Forgive me if my "good night" kisses are less frequent or my "I love you's" less present, but you should know one thing, and one only:

I'm head over heels in love with you, and out of love I write:

I love you, Dad.
I love you, Mom.

Kari

Dear Daddy,

I am writing you to tell you how I feel, to tell you how hurt my heart is feeling right now. In my house I feel alone and shut out, and you treat me the same way. One minute you want me in your life and then the next you shut me out like I don't exist. Right now I am at the point where I don't even care about life. The only thing keeping me going is the hope that in the future, life will get better for me. I am a child with a father and you make me feel as if I am a child without a father. You hardly ever call; when you do you only ask me where is my mother. You don't even ask me how I am doing. That hurts me a lot, it makes me feel as if you don't even care about me and how I am doing.

When I need money, I can't even ask you because when I do, you say, "I am going to give it to you." but I never receive it. I end up having to ask my brother's father. You always tell me you are going to do things for me but they never happen. All my life, I have depended upon my brother's father for money and support as a father. Even he, as a father, betrayed me and my trust. As a father you should have been there for me to lean on and get support from. I can't even look in your face and call you "daddy" because I have never done it before. You were never there to receive it.

You have known me for 15 years and you still, as a father, do not know my birth date, I don't even expect anything from you, but a call saying "Happy Birthday!" would be nice and it would not hurt me or you. Sometimes I sit and think: "Should I have been born or not?" I am your second oldest child and you shun me as if I am not your child at all, as if you are ashamed of me or regret having me. Do you? Do you love me or was there ever any love that you felt toward me? I think a father should at least call once in a while and say "I love you." or "I miss you, how are you doing?" You can not sit and tell me you love me because you never see me enough to grow love toward me. I understand that

you have other children, so I don't want you to support me money-wise. I just want you to act like a father toward me and not to shun me. When you feel like fitting me in your life you call me and then when you get tired of me you shun me again. I am not a yo-yo.

I have feelings too. To me you have failed as a father because being a father is not a "when you feel like it" job. It is a 24 hour job, an "around the clock" job, and you have failed years ago. But when I was young, you would call once in a while, say you were coming, and then you never showed up, you would not even call to cancel. You would just keep me waiting for you to come. You never would come, do you know how this made me feel? When in school everyone else is talking about what their fathers brought, or did for them, or where they took them, what can I say? Nothing! There is not even a time that I remember that just the two of us, you and me, spent some time together as father and daughter. I can not even tell you that I love you because I haven't seen you enough times to get to know you and come to love you as a father.

Sometimes I sit and cry wishing that the feeling I have of emptiness will go away, and my life will not seem so empty. People in school think I am such a happy person because I am almost always smiling. I smile to hide hurt and pain inside, and then, just when I can't take it anymore, I cry like a baby crying out for her mother's and father's attention and love. My mind is like a ticking alarm clock ready to go off anytime. With so many problems that I am facing in my mind, I need someone to lean on and depend on, even though I have my mother. Even she sometimes yells at me and makes me more upset than I am. So I feel "Who am I to turn to?" Leaving you with these thoughts, I hope you will write back very soon.

Sincerely,
Your daughter,

Franceen

Dear Mom,

Can you really count how many of these
letters I have written to you? I don't
think so. But this is only because there
is no way to describe how you are. Mom
I write to you today because I just wanted
you to know how much I love you.

Yesterday while I was thinking about you, I came
up with my theory of Love memories of
the four major class subjects.

In Math, I started thinking about you and said
to myself, you know, my mommy is just
like math. She gives me different ways to
figure out a problem and also adds more
happiness and subtracts loneliness
from my life every day. For example,
do you remember that day when I left for
the Dominican Republic last summer? Well,
if you remember right, I was crying. But when
I got to my plane seat I felt a letter in
my pocket from you. It said that you loved
me and to take care of my brother well while
I was gone.

In English, I said to myself, you know, my
mother does seem to have a lot in common
with English. My mom brings me poetry
to my mind. Remember that time when I
needed a poem for English, you recited
to me a poem about unity and friendship?

From that moment I realized that you were my best friend.

In Biology, I found out that my mom had much in common with biology. I am studying sexual reproduction. From that sudden moment I completely understood the process of producing a baby. The process of planting a seed of love from the lover's hand.

Although Math, English and Biology were very meaningful, I found History to be more astonishing than ever.

In History, I found out that History plays a major role in everybody's' life. And that I also owed a lot to history because if my grandmother wasn't born, then my mother wouldn't have been born and I would be the most unhappy person in the world. I love you!

S/angel

Dear parents,

How can I tell you all the fears, all the suffering, all the sorrows that worry me so much? Our future is so uncertain that we don't know what career to choose, don't know if we should bother going to school any more. How can we not worry about the unemployment rate? It does not inspire us to try hard, because it scares us. How many young women and men graduate from college with plenty of degrees but no job? How can you expect us to feel encouraged when everyone says that there are no jobs... and that our politicians can't figure out how to fix things? None of this gives us the confidence to confront the future.

How many teenagers commit suicide because they don't have the courage to confront this future that's much more than uncertain? It's downright pessimistic! The economic situation is improving, but will we be in an even worse recession in ten years? What if Clinton can't get a federal budget approved? We worry about these things also. It's our country too, you know!

Cancer, AIDS, the flesh-eating bacteria... How can we tell if these diseases will be curable in ten, twenty years? Another major source of anxiety! Oh, I wish I were Nostradamus so I could tell the future. How will it be? How will our economic and social situations evolve in the future, if the unemployment rate keeps climbing?... We can't predict these things!

War around the world disturbs us as well. It's not funny to think that one or two, or even several countries are in a state of war. When we think about the youth of these oppressed countries, how can they live in their state of total insecurity and murderous violence? How can we ignore these children's cries for help? That is something else for us to worry about, because maybe one day it will be our turn to send out the SOS.

But I want to make sure and tell you, dear parents, that thanks to you, I am eager to face the future and I want to sink my teeth into life, and most of all, I live one day at a time. Thanks to you, dear parents, I am eager to live, to go to school and study, to find a job, and to work. I say it's thanks to you because you encourage me in whatever I try, and you support me in my moments of discouragement. I know that all you want is what's best for me, and for that I thank you a thousand times over. You are truly outstanding parents! If there were more parents like you, there would definitely be less unhappiness among today's youth.

Adam

Dear Mom,

I sit here at my desk, unable to sleep. Millions of thoughts flow through my mind. I come up with things to say to you, but I am unable to express myself. I want to tell you how I feel and what I think, and when I do, you never seem to listen, or at least... understand.

I'm practically seventeen, yet still, you treat me as if I were a child. Open your eyes, Mom, and see who I really am. I'm not the baby I once was but the young woman you have raised me to be.

Every word I write is difficult; I'm perched here, like a bird trapped in its cage. I wipe away my tears of anger only for them to be replaced with tears of sadness. I continue to write my version of truth, hoping for once, you will finally understand.

I am my own person. I have a mind of my own; I am able to differentiate right from wrong. You've raised me remarkably well, but now it is time to let go and accept me for whom I am and who I want to be. Remember the Old Chinese proverb: "If you love something, set it free; if it comes back to you, it's yours; if it doesn't, it was never yours."

Mom, all I want is your respect: a respect for my freedom, privacy, and for the person I am. Some trust and understanding and love is what I need.

I'm sick and tired of you interrogating me, and not trusting me. I have never done anything to lose your trust, yet I haven't your trust and that is the trust I need so much.

I know you don't want me to make the same mistakes you made when you were my age, but you can't protect me from life forever. That's an impossible task.

You are my mother and I love you with all my heart, but it pains me not to have your trust. I guess all I'm asking is for you to love me for who I am and not try to make me the person you want me to be. I need your love more now than ever, that's something I will always need. Just let me grow up... PLEASE!

Your loving,

Sarah

Mother,

I am writing to thank you. You are not my biological mother, but to me, it's as if you were. You came into my life when I was in second grade. You always made a point of making me study and do my homework. I remember the nights when I had trouble with my multiplication tables. You made me repeat them until I knew them by heart, and when I was discouraged, you kept telling me: "One day, you'll be the president of a big corporation." You washed my clothes and fed me. Me, the best I could do was quarrel with you. I grumbled about everything and nothing: the food, the clothes and the rules. I had an answer for everything you said to me. I think I was jealous, and I was also afraid of being put in a foster home. You were so gentle when you comforted me but I didn't know how to appreciate it.

I am now a sophomore in a gifted students' program; that is a real accomplishment! And part of the accomplishment belongs to you. You have loved me as your own daughter.

I thank you. I will never forgive myself for all the tears I make you shed or that I have made you shed, but I will try to make it up to you. Mother, to you I dedicate this letter of thanks.

Sally

Dear Dad,

Hi! Last night I was thinking about you; it's hard having this big distance between us. I was wondering how things are going. I know you have been seeing your doctor almost daily for you treatments. I am worried. I just can't wait to hear your voice and know you're there.

I was sitting on my bed wondering if one day when I have children if they will be able to be held by their grandfather. I realize that since you've been ill with cancer, we've become closer and closer. I really appreciate this closeness.

I never thought cancer would hit so close to our family.

To tell you the truth, I never wrote a letter like this one before expressing my thoughts and feelings, but I hope this letter makes you feel better. I really hope your treatments make you well because I love you very much dad. I also want you to know that I'll always be here whenever you need me.

Dad, just one thing before I say good-bye. I want you to know that I love you dearly and can't wait to hold you close. I miss you very much, so please take good care of yourself and write me soon.

Your loving daughter,

Jill

To my dear parents,

You gave me life and I thought that this would be the perfect time to thank you. I'm growing up and have been learning new things on the way, but I have to tell you, it's tough being a teenager and having everything around me change. I sometimes wish that I were still a little girl, with no worries, but I thank you for guiding me along this path.

I want you to know that I realize my growing up is hard on you, because I put you through hell at times, just because something has gone wrong. It's hard on me because I later realize what I have done and I realize that everything you do is done to help me. I used to think that I had a tough family life, with all the rules and responsibilities you laid on me, but now, as I look at my friends, I am in heaven when they are going through hell. I have a great family, even though arguments arise at times, but let's face it, arguing is good for the soul.

There's one thing that I have to learn to do, and that is to express myself openly. It's so often that a topic comes up and I just walk away. It's the same when I'm in an argument: I can never argue my point, because I cannot express what I have to say. I seem to do better if I write down my feelings.

That's why I've decided to write this letter to tell both of you. No matter what happens, in good times and bad, I will always be your little girl. Growing up is hard on everybody, but we have to accept it. Please remember that I will love you till the end of time. Thanks for being such great parents and such great friends.

Loving you forever,

Elisabeth

Dear mom,

Mom, I've always wanted to do something special to tell you how I feel, because my memories of you are full of love and admiration. That's why I'm writing you today: I want to tell you that I love you very much. I am going to tell you things that I've never said before because I was too shy to express my affection for you.

Even if one day I know every language in the world, without the love you have cultivated in me, I would be like a barren field. With all the diplomas in the world, I would be nothing without your boundless love.

Mom, I would like to thank you for all the moments you were at my side. You have always been patient in difficult moments, you never even whispered a complaint: my well-being was always your first priority. Despite having your work and your own problems on your mind, you always have time to listen to me, understand me and help me find the solutions to my problems. I am sure that your love for me will last forever, and so will mine for you.

When I was a child, you weren't always there, but you responded right away to my needs; now I'm a teenager, and if I just say "mom," there you are. I assure you that I am grateful for all of that, and much more, because you give my life meaning. A thousand thanks.

I know that even if all my friends leave me, your love for me and my love for you will never fade.

I love you, mom.

Your son,

Julian

Dear Mom,

I know it's never to late to apologize, so, I found the time to do so. I don't want to just apologize, but I want a special bond between us, I want us to develop a new relationship. Starting as of now I want to take all the blame, not to show you that I favor you, but to show you I care and want to start over. He says, "When your parents forsake you he will take you into his hands..." but I know you haven't forsaken me yet, and I feel that you will never.

In your mind, you're probably thinking that I don't appreciate anything you've ever done for me, but it's not true. I maybe don't show it but I do feel your love and concern about me. Now that I'm getting the chance to show you how much I care, it would take over a million words to say. You always told me "one day I'll need the same mother that I say harmful things to, but it will be all right. I'll be there for you." Thank you for being there and everywhere.

M   - is for the million things you did for me
O   - means you're only growing old
T   - is for the tears you shed to save us
H   - is for your heart that is full of gold
E   - is for your eyes that shine like lightning
R   - means that you're right and always will be right

        and put them all together and you'll get mother.

I'm sorry for all of my disobeying.
I'm sorry for all of the stress.
I'm sorry for all the cursing.
I'm sorry, I'm sorry, I'm sorry.
What if you were to die,
would I cry?
What if you weren't a good mother,
and forsook me?
Would your love give birth to another
and choose to leave me?
But since you love me very much,
we'll develop a bond no one can touch.
So I'll pass my heart into your body
and pick up some of your burden.
Relieving the stress will help
your life to be easier to live in.
Since we're finished with that, I would like you to lead me and
show me the way to prosper in life.

"I love you, mom!"

Sincerely yours, Your son

Dear Mom & Dad,

I have always tried to be what you two wanted me to be. I have tried my utmost best to please you in every possible way. I try my best to excel in school, to stay away from people who I know you would disapprove of, and to keep my head up high. I always wanted for us to have a close relationship. And that's one of the reasons why I put out so much in making you proud. But it seems as if you aren't proud of me. No matter how hard I try, it seems to me that you see it as just what is expected of me, and nothing more. I've noticed this for a long time, but I haven't said anything to you about it. I've just kept on going in silence.

But I'm tired of the silence. I'm tired of keeping everything inside and pretending everything's fine, because it's not. Sometimes, I feel so pumped up, I think I'm just gonna explode. And there are times when I am up in my room, aching for someone to talk to, a shoulder to lean on. And oh, how I would love to run down those stairs and jump in your arms and pour out my heart to you! But I can't. And that's what hurts.

Mom and Dad, you both think you know me so well... but you don't. You don't know me at all. And do you know why you don't know me? It's because we have a lack of communication. I feel so uncomfortable talking to you. Every time we have a conversation, I begin to feel uncomfortable. Instead of concentrating on what is being said, I end up thinking about the words I must choose to say. For god's sake! I even end up wondering if my hair is fixed in a style pleasing to you, or if my clothes are OK, or even if I'm sitting correctly.

I'm sick and tired of feeling like a puppet. You guys just toy around with me. I respect and love you both very much but I think it's only fair for you guys to try understanding me, because I'm a person too. And if I can't find comfort and peace one place, then I will take the next step and look elsewhere. Do us all a favor and keep that in mind.

Your daughter

Tanya

Dear Ma,

I wish you were still alive so that I could tell you how much I love and miss you. It has been four years since you passed away. I really wish you could come back from the dead so that I could be with you.

The day you were in the hospital unconscious in a bed with all types of machines on you, I couldn't stand to be in that room seeing you suffer. And knowing I was not able to do anything for you. I went to church that day and I prayed to God that he wouldn't take you away from me. But he did! "Why?" Why couldn't he wait until I was at least fifteen. I feel that I have done something wrong in this world and I'm paying for it now.

The day your soul left the earth, I was not able to do anything for two weeks. I wanted to kill myself and leave with you. I was praying to God that he would take my life away from me so that I could be with you. I just didn't want to live. Your death was the worst thing that could have happened to me. The sad part is I lost you ma, and I was not able to tell you bye. "Why did God have to take away the only thing I've had?" You were everything to me! Sometimes I feel that there is no God. "You were the only thing I had and now you are gone."

Love,

Nilagin

Dear Parents,

Finally, I have an occasion to tell you how I feel. I have so much to tell you, I don't know where to start. First, I must talk to you separately, because that's what you are: separated. Sometimes, I hold it against you for having turned my life upside down... why can't you be like everybody else's parents? Often I want to scream out the fears and confusions that live in my mind.

You, Mom, you're so fragile and easily influenced. Why have you done this to me? Yes, you know, all those years you hurt me by swallowing pills and alcohol... All those times when you weren't you. All those times we screamed at each other loud enough to wake the dead. All those times, I wanted to run away. I was so scared... All those times I spent crying in my room. Do you remember how many times I had to go with you to the hospital in an ambulance because you had tried to put an end to your miserable existence? Why did you let yourself be influenced by that dumb religion? Why can't I be proud of my mother like everyone else?

And you, Dad, why did you never pay any attention to me? Why did you never show me your love? I need your love so much, you know... Absence is the worse form of violence one can commit against a child. Why do you prefer drugs and alcohol over me? Why don't you ever call me? And yet, I know you love me... You know, Dad, I love you too.

I would have really liked to have a normal life like other teenagers my age. It's too late now. It's impossible to go back, and I've been marked forever.

With you, Mom, it's my anger speaking sometimes. With you, Dad, I can't even talk, because I'm too shy. I'm sorry about that. At this moment, it's my heart that's speaking... My economic situation is a huge disadvantage. I do everything I can to hide it, because I feel so ashamed. It's not always easy. It's a good thing I can count on my beloved sweetheart to comfort me.

I've suffered so much from not having money that one day, you'll see, I'll have lots. That's a promise I made myself a long time ago. I want to give my children everything they might dream of... or almost everything. I don't know why all this happened to me, but soon my troubles will be over. Above all, I want you both to know I love you very much... you are my parents...

Sharron

Mom,

Do you remember, not long ago, I told you that one day I would experience perfect happiness? You said it didn't exist on earth. Well, did I tell you that I would experience it here?

I wonder if you are starting to understand. You who never understands anything. No, don't worry, I didn't run away. I certainly wouldn't want to bother you. It would be dreadful if you missed a single day of work because of me. You won't have to look for me because where I am, you can only come once... to stay.

You know, you didn't need to spell it out for me. I understood perfectly well that your work and all those men you bring home every night are more important than your family. You know, I was living in hell, so I chose to be in heaven. I must be disappointing you. Your strong little girl has lost heart. She won't be around anymore to do the housework or loan you money for your damn drugs. I damn them, but really I enjoyed them when I wanted to forget. Forget your men, your work, your drugs that got to be mine, and everything else. You never noticed that your daughter was crying inside. My heart was crying tears of blood. At this moment, I don't even hold any of this against you, because right now I'm probably floating on a cloud. I'm only asking you for one thing - not for me, but for Eve, my little darling - save her before she joins me. She really deserves to have a good life.

To end this, I send hugs and kisses to my adorable little sister. I love her and will watch over her from above. I'm giving her my old teddy bear that she wanted so much. Farewell, Eve, and take care of yourself. I love you. XXX

A girl who feels good finally,

Samantha

Dear Mom,

Since Dad has left for the Philippines, everything has been going all right. So far we've been lucky and not had to face any big problems, but if one should arise, we will definitely face it together as a family-united.

Mom, you probably don't know this but I'm scared. I'm scared for what may happen to us as a family. Dad left me in charge of things. He said when he left, "You're responsible for the family." This made me realize that from that moment, I was to be a man with responsibilities and a fear of failing you and him.

Mom, I wonder if we are financially secure even though Dad is not here. Do we have enough money to pay all our bills; if not, I am willing to work on Saturdays and Sundays to bring in a little money.

I want you to know that I love you very much and even though I don't show it; in my heart, you'll always have a place.

Your loving son,

Jonathan

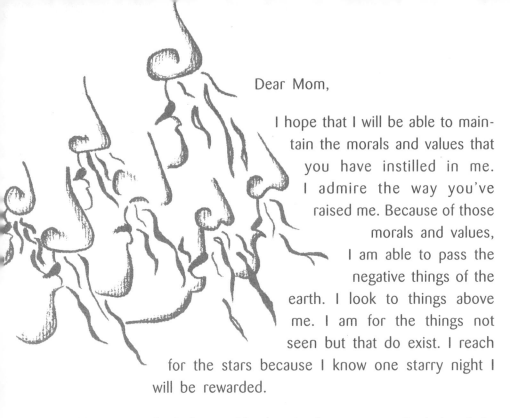

Dear Mom,

I hope that I will be able to maintain the morals and values that you have instilled in me. I admire the way you've raised me. Because of those morals and values, I am able to pass the negative things of the earth. I look to things above me. I am for the things not seen but that do exist. I reach for the stars because I know one starry night I will be rewarded.

Mom, you don't know this, but I often pray to God that I do not "turn the wrong way." I pray for strength to maintain the academic and moral standards that I set for myself, my life. I cling to the hope that through God I can conquer all. I want to make you proud to see your little girl come to be someone positive. I know that would make you most happy. Some teenagers long to be able to please their parents. Nothing they do seems to be right in the eyes of their parents. I am grateful that you have placed standards above me that I am able to reach, to grasp.

I often sit and wonder what I will be. Now I know that through God's continuous love, perseverance and your guiding hands, I will become someone both God and you will be proud of.

Love,

Kim

Dear Mom and Dad,

I am taking the time to write to the both of you and to let you know how much I love you and how much I appreciate having you as parents.

Throughout my whole life, I've been participating in many sports and if it weren't for the both of you, I wouldn't be where I am today. I sometimes have a hard time showing how I feel and maybe by writing this letter, you can get an idea of what I think and how I feel about you both.

We, as a family, have been through so much but we've always found a way to manage. The closeness in our family is the most important thing, and I cherish what we have. We sometimes get into arguments and we sometimes become frustrated but then again, isn't that normal? It's unhealthy not to argue! When I see what goes on in this world and in today's society, I consider myself lucky. I thank God for what I have and I couldn't ask for more.

To be a parent is somewhat difficult, I cannot say that I understand the position you both are in; maybe one day I will, but until then I will continue to learn from the both of you. Your patience and support means a great deal to me. Thank you for everything and I love you both.

Your future Olympian,

Tania

Dear Daddy,

I am writing this letter to tell you that I love you. I am sure that you already know this but I must tell you again. However I know that you think I am your "baby girl" but you have to believe what I am about to tell you. If you do not start to trust me, then I am not going to be a part of your life, nor you a part of mine.

I know you want the best for me, even more than what you have for yourself, but you have to understand that I will do what is right. I know that you see a lot of teenage girls with babies and boyfriends, and you start to think, "Is this what my daughter is doing?" Well, I want to reassure you that I am not.

Besides this daddy, I want to tell you that if I wanted to do anything that was wrong I would have done it already. Ridiculous curfews and the like will not stop me from doing wrong. However the knowledge that I have of what is wrong and of what is right, the love and fear of God, and love for myself and of my family members will help me to stay on the right track.

So daddy, I am going to send this letter with a little poem
I wrote for you:

Trust

Love and Trust go hand in hand.
If you love me you will understand
That you must trust me time after time,
Until I do something to change your mind.
Are you blind so as not to see
How your lack of trust keeps hurting me?
I know it's not faith in me you're lacking
But it's your trust in me that's shocking,
So even though you feel you can shelter me
One of these days I'll have to be let free.
Until that time please change your mind:
Show me the trust you could never find.

Shanequa

Dear Mom and Dad,

I'm writing this letter to get some points clear and inform you about my life, and the way I am. I am a depressed child with no life. I hide behind my music and my craziness. You know that I don't appreciate when you always say that Heavy Metal is full of hate and people that kill each other, because it isn't true. Heavy Metal is a part of my life, and much of the music expresses me. About my dressing: I love dressing like a hippie because I don't want to look like everybody else. I hate being normal and live the life I do. I wish I could go crazy before I die. I don't want to be normal! Dad, it really hurt me when you said you wouldn't walk with me anywhere because of the way I dress. I am your daughter and you should love me no matter what.

I want to inform you of something: I drink and smoke to forget my sorrow, and am currently getting high. It makes me feel good, because I know I'm not beautiful and I have the lowest self-esteem in the world. I look happy on the outside but I'm dying on the inside. I hate teenage years, they're so difficult. I wish you could understand, but I know you would never understand.

Just remember that what ever I do, I will always love you both, because you are the most important people in my life; without you I wouldn't be here. You don't like what I do to you. If something happens to me, remember that I love you.

Love always,

Consuelo

Dear Mom,

I never took time out to say this to you, but "I love you."
I love you from the bottom of my heart. I love the way you
smile at me whenever I achieve one of my many goals. I love
the way you always try to cheer me up whenever I am down.
I love the way you stay up late at night to help me study for
my exams or just to ensure that my homework is done. This
means so much to me because it shows me that you care.

I know you care a lot for me because you take time away from
your busy schedule just to be with me. Your love for me shows
when you walk away from your job "to look after your daughter's
business" or use most of you paycheck to "put on a special
party for your daughter's birthday." Those little deeds add up
to a grand total in my heart.

I am happy when you come home with a smile on your face,
and sad when you come home down. Sometimes you don't know
it, but what you feel is what I feel. Your love runs from you
into me. Because of the love I receive at home, I am able to
love the people I encounter. You are a big part of my life and
you will always be a diamond, a jewel in the eyes of this, your
child. Everyday, I thank God for you.

Love,

Kim-Marie

Notes between the egg and the sky

Authors and illustrators wanted!

According to our experience, every teenager possesses several talents. At Between Us Publishing, we are interested in two. We search for teenagers who like to play with pen and pencil, who like to write or draw. If you are one of these, we invite you to submit your texts and illustrations to us.

Presently we are preparing two books. One is titled **"Dear grandfather, dear grandmother"**; the other, **"Dear teachers."** If you would like to submit one or several letters for these books, mail them to us. Make sure to identify every text with your *name, address, and phone number.* If your text is chosen you will be paid as an author: 10% of net sales, like the young authors who were published in **"Dear parents."**

For a series titled BETWEEN US, we are looking for illustrators. Send us three illustrations or caricatures, in a humorous or serious style, staring teenagers facing situations of indecision, where they don't know what to choose or what to do. The illustrations must be in black and white, in one of the following formats:

2" x 2", 2" x 4", or 4" x 4".

Identify thoroughly each illustrations.

If you are a parent, a teacher or the principal of a school, we would also be happy to read your work. Two other books for the series LETTERS are being prepared: **"Dear students"** and **"Dear daughter, dear son."** We would appreciate receiving your letters. If yours is chosen, you will also be remunerated as an author.

Soon we are going to launch a site on the Internet. The Between Us site will be for teenagers. A place where you can meet and exchange, where you can talk about what interests you: friends, school, the future, first love, music, movies, stars, fears, government, war, girls, boys, shyness, anger, loneliness, etc. On the site, you can learn about our authors and illustrators, leave them questions and comments via email.

You can also share your writing with other teens. There will be a section for science fiction, poetry, love stories, horror stories, jokes, adventures and essays. If you want to be kept informed about our activities, and upcoming contests and books, you will be able to leave your snail mail or email address on the site. We are open to suggestions. This site is for you. If you want us to send you the web address when it opens, email us at bahl@cam.org.

Notes between the egg and the sky

Contest
"Can you catch a spelling mistake?"

We didn't modify the style of our young authors but we did correct the spelling mistakes that might have been in their letters. We hope we didn't miss any. If you discover one, please notify us; we would appreciate it greatly. By doing so, you'll become eligible to win a book of your choice published by Between Us Publishing. Copy the sentence containing the spelling mistake, while correcting it. Under it mention the title of the book, "Dear parents", the page where the mistake is, your name, address, age and phone number. Each participant can enter the same mistake only once. A winner will be chosen by a random drawing each two months: the fifteenth of February, April, June, August, October, and December, of 1996, 1997 and 1998. Each entry will be kept for one year. To obtain a copy of the winners and the rules of this contest, send a self-addressed, prestamped envelop to Between Us Publishing inc.

Get to know us, let us know you.

Each time we organize a contest or come out with a new book, we send a newsletter or a media communiqué to different organizations and individuals: high school newspapers, parent associations, psychologists, therapists, counselors, youth organizations, English teachers, family centers, etc. If you are not on our list, and would like to be kept informed of our activities, write to us at one of our addresses, found on page two. Give us your name, title, profession and the name of your association (if it applies), your address, city, state (or province), phone number, fax number and email address (if you have one). If you represent an organization, send us some brochures and documents explaining what you do in your community. We will be happy to hear about your needs and keep you informed in the future about our projects.

Friends, Readers,

I have created Between Us Publishing for you, to give you a media in which your voice can be heard. I greatly appreciate your support of our efforts by buying this book, for thus we will be able to develop and print others, with the same goal of building bridges between us by presenting the perspectives of each, with respect and without judgement.

There is no good, nor bad;
        no success, or failure.
There are different potentials,
        different people,
whose differences are beautiful!

I would love to know if this book touched, helped or pleased you, but also if certain aspects of the content and style left you puzzled or unsatisfied. Do not hesitate to share your comments with my team and I. They are precious to us. The addresses to which you can send your comments are on page two.

Thank you for reading these teenagers, and be reassured that even the most desperate authors in this collection are still with us today.

I want to take advantage of the lines that remain to thank all those who worked benevolently on the production of this book: David R. S., Johan L., Linda D., Andrew B., Suzan D. B., Benoit C., Mark-Andrew B., Lucy S., Martine R., Julie M., Tamara E-H, etc. Also, thanks to all the teachers who answered our call and encouraged their students to write for us. Many thanks to the parents who read the manuscript of this book and thus enabled us to make precious final adjustments before publication.

Thanks to all! I appreciate your help greatly!

Hope to see you soon,

Sonia Bahl
Publisher